Basic Skills for the
TOEFL® iBT

Moraig Macgillivray
Kayang Gagiano

Compass
Publishing

Reading 1

Basic Skills for the TOEFL® iBT 1
Reading

Kayang Gagiano | Moraig Macgillivray

© 2008 Compass Publishing

Project Editor: Liana Robinson
Acquisitions Editor: Emily Page
Content Editor: Michael Jones
Copy Editor: Erik Custer
Contributing Writers: Edaan Getzel, Jeff Zeter
Consultants: Lucy Han, Chanhee Park
Cover/Interior Design: Dammora Inc

email: info@compasspub.com
http://www.compasspub.com

ISBN: 978-1-59966-153-7

19 18 17 16 15 14
17 16 15 14

Printed in Korea

Contents

Introduction to the TOEFL® iBT

What is the TOEFL® test?

The TOEFL® iBT test (Test of English as a Foreign Language Internet-based test) is designed to assess English proficiency in non-native speakers who want to achieve academic success as well as effective communication. It is not meant to test academic knowledge or computer ability; therefore, questions are always based on material found in the test.

The TOEFL® iBT test is divided into four sections:
- Reading
- Speaking
- Listening
- Writing

TOEFL® Scores

TOEFL® scores can be used for:
- Admission into university or college where instruction is in English
- Employers or government agencies who need to determine a person's English ability
- English-learning institutes which need to place students in the appropriate level of English instruction

It is estimated that about 4,400 universities and other institutions require a certain TOEFL® test score for admission.

The exact calculation of a TOEFL® test score is complicated and not necessary for the student to understand. However, it is helpful to know that:
- Each section in the Internet-based test is worth 30 points
- The highest possible score on the iBT is 120 points
- Each institution will have its own specific score requirements

✱ It is very important to check with each institution individually to find out what its admission requirements are.

Registering for the TOEFL® iBT

Students who wish to take the TOEFL® test must get registration information. Registration information can be obtained online at the ETS website. The Internet address is www.ets.org/toefl.

The website provides information such as:
- testing locations
- identification requirements
- registration information
- costs
- other test preparation material
- test center locations

This information will vary depending on the country in which you take the test. Be sure to follow the requirements carefully. If you do not have the proper requirements in order, you may not be able to take the test. Remember that if you register online, you will need to have your credit card information ready.

Introduction to the Reading Section of the TOEFL® iBT

In the reading section of the TOEFL® test, you will be required to read 3-5 passages on varying topics. After each passage, you will answer 12-14 questions that test your ability to:

- understand vocabulary
- recognize sentence structure
- determine factual information
- determine implied information
- recognize the writer's intention

You will not be permitted to see the questions until after you have read the passage. While answering the questions, you will be permitted to look back at the reading. You do not need any previous knowledge on the topic in order to answer the questions correctly.

Passage Types:

1. Exposition—material that provides information about or an explanation of a topic
2. Argumentation—material that presents a point of view about a topic and provides supporting evidence in favor of a position
3. Narrative—an account of a person's life or a historical event

Reading Question Types:

Most questions will be multiple-choice questions. The following list explains the types and number of each type of question per passage. Questions may not appear in this order.

Question Type	Number	Description
Vocabulary	3-4	Choose the best meaning of a word or phrase
Reference	0-1	Identify the noun to which a pronoun is referring
Factual Information	2-4	Select details or facts provided in the passage
Negative Fact	1	Identify details or facts NOT provided, or NOT true according to the passage
Sentence Simplification	1	Choose the best answer to demonstrate your understanding of a sentence and your ability to analyze its meaning
Inference	0-1	Draw an inference from the passage by choosing an answer that is not actually said in the passage, but is implied or can be inferred
Rhetorical Purpose	1-2	Identify why the writer has mentioned something in a certain way or in a certain place
Insert Text	1	Insert a sentence into the most appropriate place in the passage
Summary	0-1	Choose the sentences that best summarize the entire passage
Table	0-1	Categorize major ideas or important information from the passage

Most questions are worth 1 point each, however Summary questions are worth 2 points and Table questions are worth 3-4 points.

Test management:

- Questions cannot be viewed until after the passage has been read.
- You can return to previous questions you may wish to revise or recheck by using the Review icon at the top of the screen.
- You will be allowed to study the reading as you attempt the questions.
- There is a glossary included for some words.
- When reading passages, ask yourself the following important questions:
  - ⇨ What is the main idea of the passage?
  - ⇨ How is the main idea developed/supported in the passage?
  - ⇨ What is the main point/role of each paragraph?
- You have 60-100 minutes to read the passages and answer 12-14 questions per passage. This usually means approximately 20 minutes per passage and set of questions. Try to pace yourself accordingly. The recommended reading speed would be approximately 100-150 words per minute. Therefore, you should try to read the passages in this book at that speed.
- For each set of questions, first answer all of the questions that you can answer easily. You can then go back and answer questions that are more difficult if you have time.

Introduction to the *Basic Skills for the TOEFL® iBT* series

***Basic Skills for the TOEFL® iBT* is a 3-level, 12-book test preparation series designed for beginning-level students of the TOEFL® iBT.** Over the course of the series, students build on their current vocabulary to include common TOEFL® and academic vocabulary. They are also introduced to the innovative questions types found on the TOEFL® iBT, and are provided with practice of TOEFL® iBT reading, listening, speaking, and writing passages, conversations, lectures, and questions accessible to students of their level.

***Basic Skills for the TOEFL® iBT* enables students to build on both their language skills and their knowledge.** The themes of the passages, lectures, and questions cover the topics often seen on the TOEFL® iBT. In addition, the independent topics, while taking place in a university setting, are also accessible to and understood by students preparing to enter university. The academic topics are also ones that native speakers study.

Students accumulate vocabulary over the series. Vocabulary learned at the beginning of the series will appear in passages and lectures later in the book, level, and series. Each level gets progressively harder. The vocabulary becomes more difficult, the number of vocabulary words to be learned increases, and the passages and lectures get longer and increase in level. By the end of the series, students will know all 570 words on the standard Academic Word List (AWL) used by TESOL and have a solid foundation in and understanding of the TOEFL® iBT.

Not only will *Basic Skills for the TOEFL® iBT* start preparing students for the TOEFL® iBT, but it will also give students a well-rounded basis for either further academic study in English or further TOEFL® iBT study.

Introduction to the *Basic Skills for the TOEFL® iBT* Reading Book

This book is the first in the *Basic Skills for the TOEFL® iBT* series. Each unit has three passages relating to an overall topic. This introduces students to the topics they will see in the other three books—Listening, Speaking, and Writing—in level one.

Each unit is separated into four sections:

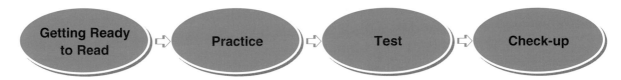

The following will outline the activities and aims of each section.

Getting Ready to Read

Key Vocabulary and TOEFL Vocabulary

Students begin by studying the vocabulary they will encounter in the following passage.
TOEFL® Vocabulary is the words that have been found to appear most often in TOEFL® preparation materials or are Academic Word List (AWL) words. TOEFL® Vocabulary is the most important words for the student to learn in order to build their vocabulary before further TOEFL® study. **Key Vocabulary** is the other words that are important for the student to know in order to understand the passage that will follow.

TOEFL Question Types

In this part, students will become familiar with:
- one or two of the question types that appear in the TOEFL® iBT Reading section
- the common wording and the aims of the question types
- the strategy for identifying a question type

Becoming familiar with the question types is important for the student, as it will help them answer the questions appropriately. Therefore, the student will be less likely to get confused or distracted by the wording of TOEFL® questions.

Over the course of the book, all the reading question types will be covered.

Reading Passage

This is the first passage of the unit. It contains the vocabulary words learned on the previous page and there should be no words that student is unfamiliar with. This helps students become used to reading academic type passages but at a level they can understand. Students are asked to number each paragraph of the passage with the correct main idea or purpose. This enables them to become used to thinking about not only the passage in general but also what the main idea is and how that main idea is developed and supported throughout the passage.

Note-taking

The next part is a summary. The blanks in the summary are facts that important to the understanding of the passage and are often also either Key or TOEFL® Vocabulary. This helps students visualize the organization of the passage and prepares students to take their own notes during the real TOEFL® test.

TOEFL Questions

The next page gives students the opportunity to practice the question types they were introduced to on the first page of the unit. There will be two of each question type and they will be worded in the same way as they are in the real TOEFL® test.

TOEFL Vocabulary Practice

The next part is sentences using the TOEFL® Vocabulary the student learned at the beginning of the section. This helps students practice the words in context.

Practice

Key Vocabulary and TOEFL Vocabulary

This is the Key Vocabulary and TOEFL® Vocabulary they will encounter in following passage. See previous section for a full explanation.

Reading Passage

Students read the second passage of the unit. The passage contains the vocabulary words learned above. The students should underline the key information. This is again to help the student with identifying the main idea and how that main idea is developed and supported throughout the passage.

TOEFL Questions

This part gives students the opportunity to practice each question type they were introduced to in this unit and in the previous unit. They are worded in the same way as they are in the real TOEFL® test.

TOEFL Vocabulary Practice

The next part is sentences using the TOEFL® Vocabulary the student learned at the beginning of the section. This helps students practice the words in context.

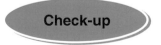

Test

The test contains the last and longest passage of the unit. It is similar to the real TOEFL® test, but at an appropriate level for the student. It gives the student the opportunity to practice many question types at the same time. The test passage also uses many of the vocabulary words learned over the course of the unit.

Check-up

Question Type Review

These questions check the student understands the aim of question type that was focused on throughout the unit.

Key Vocabulary Practice

This part is sentences using the Key vocabulary the student learned over the course of the unit. This helps students practice the words in context.

Basic Skills for the TOEFL® iBT

Reading Lesson Plan - 50 minutes

Homework Check	5 min.	• Talk about any homework questions that the students did not understand. A combination of both teacher and peer explanations should be used.
Review	10 min.	• Review the strategies discussed in the previous unit and talk about other strategies students might have employed when they did homework. • Have a few students give oral summary of the passages they read for homework. ✷ If the test section was not given as homework it should be completed here.
Main Lesson	30 min.	**Getting Ready to Read** A. Learn the words • Preview the vocabulary and have students read the words aloud. • Have students predict the topic of the first passage. • Talk about what parts of speech the words belong to. ✷ Vocabulary preview can also be done immediately before the first reading passage. B. Learn the question types • Introduce the TOEFL® question types. • Discuss strategies that can be applied to the question types. C. Reading Passage • Ask the students to read the passage within a given time (about 1 minute.) • Talk about the main points and the organization of the passage as a class. D. Note-taking • Have students fill in the summary in pairs or in groups. • Ask students to write a few questions using the target question types. E. TOEFL Questions • Ask students to do the questions. Then as a class or in pairs talk about the strategies they used to answer the questions. • Ask students to make another question, using the target question type, by themselves or in pairs. They should then ask their peers to answer the question. F. TOEFL Vocabulary Practice • Ask students to complete the sentences and check their answers in pairs. **Practice** A. Learn the words • Preview the vocabulary and have students read the words aloud. • Talk about what parts of speech the words belong to.
Wrap-up	5 min.	• Check the strategies • Give homework (the rest of the Practice section) ✷ The Test section and Check-up section can also be given as homework.

Teaching Tips

- In the real TOEFL® iBT Reading Section, each reading passage has the title above it, so students are encouraged to read the title first and predict what the passage is about.

- It is strongly recommended to teach the target vocabulary prior to reading.

- It is a good idea to have students make their own vocabulary list on their PC or notebook. Putting the words under thematic categories (categories of subjects) would be an effective way to study the words.

- It is important to emphasize understanding of the main idea of the passage. Students often read the passage without constructing the framework of the passage, which could cause them problems understanding the main points later.

- Note-taking practice needs to be done in class with the teacher's assistance in the beginning because not many students are familiar with note-taking. Gradually, have students take notes in groups, pairs, and then individually.

- At least one passage and the following questions should be done as an in-class activity; otherwise, students will not be able to understand the strategies and the new information.

- It is important to have the students read through the passage quickly (skim).

- Timed-reading is an effective activity. Teachers can change the time limit as students' reading speed builds up. Do the same with the comprehension questions.

- Encourage students to do timed-reading even when they do their homework. It is a good idea to record the time they read on their book.

- Written and oral summary is recommended as the real TOEFL® iBT includes the summary question. In addition, it is a useful exercise to prepare for the Speaking and Writing sections.

- Students can use the definitions and synonyms in the vocabulary section when they summarize or paraphrase the passages.

- Use the test at the end of each unit as a progress check by keeping recording the scores of the tests.

[01] History

Getting Ready to Read

A. Learn the words.

Key Vocabulary

well-known	famous; talked about
factory	a place where goods are made, usually by machines
cruel	willfully causing pain or distress

TOEFL Vocabulary

leader	the head of a nation, political party, or other group of people
impact	a strong effect or influence
nation	a country
agriculture	the practice of farming or growing crops
industry	the practice of manufacturing goods

B. Learn the question types.

TOEFL Question Types

Vocabulary

The word X in the passage is closest in meaning to . . .
In stating X, the author means that . . .

- This type of question asks for the meaning of a word or phrase in the context of how it is used in the passage.
- The word is usually important to understanding part of the passage.

Reference

The word X in the passage refers to . . .

- This type of question asks for what a word or phrase is referring to.
- The word is often a pronoun.

C. Read the passage. Number each paragraph with the correct main idea or purpose.

> 1. The writer's opinion of Stalin
> 2. Information about changes Stalin made in the Soviet Union
> 3. What the passage is about
> 4. Information about Stalin's name change

Joseph Stalin

___Joseph Stalin is a well-known leader. He was the leader of the Soviet Union from 1928 until 1953.

___When he was born, he was called Iosif Dzhugashvili. Later he changed his name to Stalin. The word "Stalin" means "man of steel" in Russian. Stalin chose this new name so that people would think of him as a strong leader.

___Stalin had a big impact on the Soviet Union. He changed the country. It went from a nation based on agriculture to one based on industry. He forced thousands of farm workers to leave their farms. He made them move to the cities to work in factories.

___Stalin was cruel. He killed many people to get what he wanted.

D. Complete the summary notes by filling in the blanks.

Topic: Joseph Stalin

Introduction: _____ leader of the Soviet Union from 1928 to _____.

Name: Called _____ Dzhugashvili.

Changed his name to _____.

Means "man of _____" in Russian.

Wanted people to think he was a _____ leader.

Impact: _____ the country.

• From a _____ based on _____

• To a nation based on _____

Forced farm _____ to work in _____.

Conclusion: Was _____.

Killed many to get what he wanted.

E. Choose the correct answers.

1. The word he in the passage refers to
   (A) Joseph Stalin   (B) the farm workers

2. The word strong in the passage is closest in meaning to
   (A) powerful   (B) healthy

3. The word it in the passage refers to
   (A) industry   (B) the Soviet Union

4. The word forced in the passage is closest in meaning to
   (A) made   (B) hit

TOEFL Vocabulary Practice

F. Fill in the blanks with the correct words.

leader	impact	nation	agriculture	industry

1. Russia has more land than any other _____.

2. Detroit is famous for its car _____.

3. President Bill Clinton was the _____ of the United States from 1993 to 2001.

4. Taking vitamins has a good _____ on my health.

5. Growing fruits and vegetables is an example of _____.

Practice

A. Learn the words.

Key Vocabulary

ruins	the pieces that are left from very old buildings or cities
pottery	objects made of baked clay
mine	a hole in the earth for collecting valuable materials

TOEFL Vocabulary

consist	to be made of
archaeologist	someone who studies items from long ago
conclusion	a decision
trade	buying and selling or exchanging goods
resource	something we can use; something that helps us

B. Read the passage and underline the key information.

Great Zimbabwe Ruins

There is a country in Africa called Zimbabwe. It has many large, old buildings. Some of these buildings are called the *Great Zimbabwe Ruins*. Sometimes, they are called *The Houses of Stone*. They consist of hundreds of stone ruins.

The ruins were found by Portuguese people in 1531. Nobody had lived in the buildings for many years. It is not known why people left this place.

Archaeologists studied the ruins in the 1800s. They wanted to learn more about them. They found many Arabian coins. They also found a lot of Chinese pottery. The coins and pottery were found near the ruins. They came to the conclusion that the people who had lived there traded with other nations.

There are many gold mines near the ruins. Archaeologists think the Arabian and Chinese people wanted the gold. That is why they traded with the people in Zimbabwe. The gold was a very good trading resource.

C. Choose the correct answers.

1. The word they in the passage refers to

(A) Portuguese people   (B) archaeologists

2. The word ruins in the passage is closest in meaning to

(A) old buildings   (B) African stones

3. According to the passage, the Zimbabwe ruins can be found

(A) in America   (B) in Africa

4. According to the passage, scientists found all of these items EXCEPT

(A) Arabian coins

(B) African beads

(C) Chinese pottery

TOEFL Vocabulary Practice

D. Fill in the blanks with the correct words.

| consists | conclusion | archaeologists | traded | resource |

1. Steel is an important _____.

2. _____ often go to very old places to learn about the people who lived there.

3. The police officer came to the _____ that the man had robbed the bank.

4. Greek salad _____ of tomato, cucumber, and feta cheese.

5. The diamonds mined in South Africa are _____ for money.

Read the passage.

The Slave Trade

Slaves were people. However, they were owned by other people. Slaves had to work very hard for no money. Many people in the United States owned slaves. Slaves were used for almost 250 years.

Slaves were traded in the United States. This started around 1619. Dutch people sold slaves from Africa. Many American farmers bought the slaves. The slaves were a good resource because they had to work hard. They were also very cheap. They were cheap because the farmers didn't have to pay them.

Many slaves worked in agriculture. In some parts of the United States, the slaves grew crops. The crops consisted of tobacco and cotton. The farmers became rich.

The impact of slavery was good for the farmers. They made a lot of money. The impact on the slaves was very bad. They were not free. They could not go where they wanted. They could not choose their work. They also had no money.

At first, Americans thought slavery was good. Many people owned slaves. Rich people had a lot of slaves. ■ 1) Slave owners were cruel. They stopped slaves from running away. ■ 2) They often hit them and hurt their families. ■ 3) The slaves were scared, so they didn't run away. ■ 4)

Finally, many Americans came to the conclusion that slavery was bad. Slavery ended in 1865. A well-known American leader ended it. His name was Abraham Lincoln. He freed the slaves.

Choose the correct answers.

1. According to the passage, slaves are

   (A) always women
   (B) farmers who are rich
   (C) people who are forced to work for no money
   (D) people who are happy to work hard

2. The word owned in the passage is closest in meaning to

   (A) take   (B) sell
   (C) have   (D) want

3. Which of the following best expresses the essential information in the highlighted sentences? Incorrect answers change the meaning in important ways or leave out essential information.

Slaves were traded in America. This started around 1619.

(A) Americans were working as slaves by 1619.
(B) Slaves wanted to work in America in 1619.
(C) By 1619, Americans were ending the slave trade.
(D) In 1619, the USA started the slave trade.

4. Look at the four squares (■) that indicate where the following sentence could be added to the passage.

Sometimes they even killed the slaves who made them angry.

Where would the sentence best fit?

(A) Square 1   (B) Square 2
(C) Square 3   (D) Square 4

5. What can be inferred about President Abraham Lincoln?

(A) He thought slavery was bad.   (B) He died in 1865.
(C) He was a slave owner.   (D) He was a slave.

6. **Directions:** An introductory sentence for a brief summary of the passage is provided below. Complete the summary by selecting the THREE answer choices that express the most important ideas in the passage. Some sentences do not belong in the summary because they express ideas that are not presented in the passage or are minor ideas in the passage.

Slavery existed in the United States from 1619 until 1865.

Answer choices

(A) The slaves' wishes came true when President Lincoln freed them.
(B) Rich Americans owned many slaves.
(C) American farmers became rich by using slave labor.
(D) Dutch traders sold many slaves to Americans.
(E) Slaves were usually very badly treated and wished to be free.

Check-up

A. Choose the correct answers.

1. A *vocabulary* question asks

   (A) what a word or phrase means
   (B) what a word or phrase doesn't mean
   (C) what a word or phrase refers to
   (D) what another meaning of a word or phrase is

2. A *reference* question asks

   (A) what a word or phrase means
   (B) what a word or phrase doesn't refer to
   (C) what a word or phrase doesn't mean
   (D) what a word or phrase refers to

Key Vocabulary Practice

B. Fill in the blanks with the correct words.

well-known	factory	cruel	ruins	pottery	mines

1. Televisions are made in a _____.

2. Mickey Mouse is a _____ cartoon character.

3. People dig in _____ to get gold.

4. You should not be _____ to animals.

5. The tomb of King Tutankhamen contained a lot of _____.

6. The pyramids in Egypt are very famous _____.

[02] Art

Getting Ready to Read

A. Learn the words.

Key Vocabulary

modern art	art created from the mid-19th century
tired	no longer interested
canvas	strong cloth that artists paint on

TOEFL Vocabulary

century	a time period of 100 years
imagine	to create an idea or image in the mind
inspire	to cause or bring about
odd	not regular; unusual
formal	following the correct ways; official

B. Learn the question types.

TOEFL Question Types

Factual Information

According to the author, X did Y because . . .

According to the passage, X occurred because . . .

The author's description of X mentions which of the following?

- This type of question asks about specific facts or details.
- The answer is always directly stated somewhere in the passage.

Negative Factual Information

According to the passage, which of the following is NOT true of X?

The author's description of X mentions all of the following EXCEPT . . .

- This type of question asks which fact or detail does NOT appear in the passage or is NOT correct.
- The other answer choices are usually directly stated somewhere in the passage.

C. Read the passage. Number each paragraph with the correct main idea or purpose.

> 1. Opinions of modern art
> 2. What modern art looked like
> 3. Why modern art began
> 4. Where art comes from

Modern Art

___Art comes from the imagination. In the 19th century, some painters imagined new ways to paint. They inspired a new kind of art—modern art.

___Modern art began when some painters were tired of painting the same way. Most people thought paintings should look real. However, these painters made people and other things look odd.

___How did the painters do this? Some used odd colors. Others threw paint on canvases. Later, one even painted things like soup cans.

___At first, people did not like this kind of art. They thought art should look formal. Then, things changed. Many people began to understand and like modern art.

D. Complete the summary notes by filling in the blanks.

Topic:	Modern Art
Introduction:	Art comes from the _____.
	In the 19th _____ painters _____ new ways to paint.
Beginnings:	Painters were _____ of painting the same way.
	Most thought paintings should look _____.
	Painters made people and things look _____.
Painting styles:	Some used odd _____.
	Others threw _____ on canvases.
	Others painted things like _____.
People's thoughts:	At first, people _____ like this kind of art.
	Then, people began to _____ and like modern art.

E. Choose the correct answers.

1. According to the passage, which is true of art?

(A) Art comes from the imagination.

(B) All art is modern.

2. According to the passage, modern art began because

(A) people were tired of looking at the same paintings

(B) some painters were tired of painting in the same ways

3. According to the passage which of the following is NOT true of modern art?

(A) Painters started it in the 19th century.

(B) People said it was too formal.

4. The author's description of modern art mentions all of the following EXCEPT

(A) at first, people loved it

(B) modern art made people and other things look odd

(C) some modern artists threw paint on canvases

TOEFL Vocabulary Practice

F. Fill in the blanks with the correct words.

century	inspire	imagine	odd	formal

1. Many famous painters had no _____ art education.

2. The first airplane flew in the 20th _____.

3. Most artists _____ their paintings before they begin to paint.

4. The works of famous modern artists like Picasso and Matisse still _____ artists today.

5. Some people think the modern art makes people and things look _____.

Practice

A. Learn the words.

Key Vocabulary

stroke	a line made with a paintbrush or pen
dot	a very small round mark
pure	nothing mixed in

TOEFL Vocabulary

introduce	to present for the first time
blend	to mix together
normal	regular; usual
pose	to hold your body in a certain position
style	a way of doing something

B. Read the passage and underline the key information.

Georges Seurat

Georges Seurat was born in 1859. He was a French painter. He studied art like a science. He knew a lot about colors and light. He introduced a way of painting no one had ever seen.

Seurat's paintings looked different. He did not paint with big strokes. He put many, very small dots on the canvas instead. Some paintings were made of millions of dots.

Another difference was the way he used color. Most artists blended their paints. However, Seurat did not. He used only pure paint colors. This odd use of color made his paintings shimmer.

Also, the people in his paintings were just doing normal things. They weren't posing. This did not look like normal art.

Seurat died in 1891. He was young when he died. He was only 31. His different style made him a well-known modern artist.

C. Choose the correct answers.

1. The word shimmer in the passage is closest in meaning to

(A) shine   (B) age

2. The word they in the passage refers to

(A) people who looked at the paintings

(B) people in the paintings

3. According to the passage, which of the following is true about the people in Seurat's paintings?

(A) The people all knew each other.

(B) The people were doing normal things.

4. According to the passage, which of the following is NOT true about Seurat's painting style?

(A) He used only pure paint colors.

(B) He used normal brush strokes.

TOEFL Vocabulary Practice

D. Fill in the blanks with the correct words.

normal	blend	introduce	pose	style

1. Georges Seurat did not have people _____ for his paintings.

2. Some artists _____ their paints.

3. Georges Seurat liked to paint pictures of people doing _____ things.

4. Many museums offer lessons to _____ children to modern art.

5. Many artists have their own _____ of painting.

Read the passage.

Renaissance Art

Renaissance art was a new kind of art. It was different from art before it. The Renaissance was a time of change. People were learning more. They understood math. They knew more about science. This knowledge was introduced in their art.

Before this time, people did not think artists were special. Artists were normal people. They were not trained. Their paintings did not look real. However, artists in the 16th century had more training. They understood lines, light, and shadow. They knew how to blend science with art. Their paintings looked very real. Some thought their paintings were perfect.

Before the Renaissance, artists mostly painted people from the Bible. ■ 1) When the Renaissance started, artists began to paint different people. ■ 2) Also, they painted many objects. They put a lot of detail in their paintings. Michelangelo and Raphael were two well-known artists of the time. ■ 3) They inspired people with their art. ■ 4)

At this time, people thought artists were special people. They thought they were God-like. They became important people. This meant that many more people wanted to see the well-known artists' paintings.

Also, around this time, the printing press started to be used. This meant that copies of Renaissance paintings were made. These copies were sent all over the world. People everywhere were amazed at this art. Today millions of people travel to see this special art. Many people still think this style of art is perfect.

Choose the correct answers.

1. Which of the following best expresses the essential information in the highlighted sentence? Incorrect answers change the meaning in important ways or leave out essential information.

   They knew how to blend science with art.

   (A) Artists used science to make their art better.
   (B) Art was used to make science better.
   (C) Artists were not interested in science.
   (D) Scientists were interested in art.

2. Which of the following can be inferred about artists before the 16ᵗʰ century?

(A) They understood light and shadow.
(B) They had a lot of training.
(C) They were very good painters.
(D) They didn't know much about science.

3. The word they in the passage refers to

(A) people
(B) artists
(C) Michelangelo and Raphael
(D) people from the Bible

4. Look at the four squares (■) that indicate where the following sentence could be added to the passage.

Michelangelo's paintings are some of the most well-known paintings in the world.

Where would the sentence best fit?

(A) Square 1
(C) Square 3
(B) Square 2
(D) Square 4

5. According to paragraph 5, all of the following are true about Renaissance art EXCEPT

(A) copies of this art was sent all over the world
(B) the printing press helped artists paint more
(C) many people still think of Renaissance art as perfect
(D) many people travel to see this artwork today

6. Directions: An introductory sentence for a brief summary of the passage is provided below. Complete the summary by selecting the THREE answer choices that express the most important ideas in the passage. Some sentences do not belong in the summary because they express ideas that are not presented in the passage or are minor ideas in the passage.

Renaissance art was different from art before it.

Answer choices

(A) Renaissance paintings looked real.
(B) People thought Renaissance artists were not clever.
(C) Renaissance artists were not trained.
(D) Renaissance artists knew more about math and science.
(E) People thought Renaissance artists were special.

Check-up

A. Choose the correct answers.

1. *A factual information* question asks

    (A) about specific details or facts that are in the passage
    (B) what a word or phrase refers to
    (C) what a word or phrase means
    (D) about details or facts that are NOT in the passage

2. *A negative factual* information question asks

    (A) what a word or phrase refers to
    (B) about specific details or facts that are in the passage
    (C) about details or facts that are NOT in the passage
    (D) what a word or phrase means

Key Vocabulary Practice

B. Fill in the blanks with the correct words.

dot	strokes	pure	canvas	tired	modern art

1. The world's largest painting is on a _____ that measures 100 meters by 12 meters.

2. It took Seurat two years to paint his most famous painting because he painted it one _____ at a time.

3. _____ started in the mid-19th century.

4. Up, down, left, or right are common brush _____ in painting.

5. Some artists mix colors but others like to use _____ colors.

6. Modern artists were _____ of the old methods of painting.

[03] Zoology

Getting Ready to Read

A. Learn the words.

Key Vocabulary

fur	hair on an animal
hunt	to follow an animal to kill it
blend in	to be difficult to see from similar things around

TOEFL Vocabulary

extreme	farthest out, severe
surroundings	area around
determine	to decide something
opportunity	favorable situation
attack	to hurt with violence

B. Learn the question type.

TOEFL Question Type

Sentence Simplification
Which of the following best expresses the essential information in the highlighted sentence?
Incorrect answers change the meaning in important ways or leave out essential information.

- This type of question asks for the answer that best restates, summarizes, or simplifies a sentence from the passage.
- The answer will use different vocabulary or grammar and it will often use synonyms.

C. Read the passage. Number each paragraph with the correct main idea or purpose.

1. How the bear gets its food
2. Where polar bears live
3. What the bear likes to eat
4. What the white fur does to help the bear

Polar Bears

___Giant polar bears have beautiful white fur. They live near the North Pole in extreme weather.

___There is not much food at the North Pole. Polar bears like to hunt seals, but it is hard to find seals to hunt. Therefore, polar bears often have to eat other animals. When they do find seals, they have to hunt them carefully.

___The white fur helps polar bears blend in with their surroundings. Because it is the same color as the snow, it's hard to determine where the bear is.

___When the bear has an opportunity, it will attack a seal. Seals usually cannot see polar bears in time. The attack is usually a surprise for them. It is their white fur that helps polar bears hunt.

D. Complete the summary notes by filling in the blanks.

Topic:	Polar Bears
Introduction:	Have white _____.
	Live near the _____ in _____ weather.
Food:	Not much _____.
	Like to _____ seals but hard to find.
	Often eat other _____.
	Have to hunt _____.
White fur:	White fur helps to _____ with surroundings.
	White fur is same color as _____.
Hunting:	When it has an opportunity, the bear will _____ a seal.
	• Cannot see bears in _____
	• _____ for them
	White fur helps polar bears _____.

E. Choose the correct answers.

1. Which of the following best expresses the essential information in the highlighted sentence? Incorrect answers change the meaning in important ways or leave out essential information.

The white fur helps polar bears blend in with their surroundings.

(A) The white fur helps polar bears hide.

(B) The fur helps confuse bears.

2. Which of the following best expresses the essential information in the highlighted sentence? Incorrect answers change the meaning in important ways or leave out essential information.

Because it is the same color as the snow, it's hard to determine where the bear is.

(A) Because polar bears are white, it is easy to find them.

(B) The bear and snow are the same color, so it is hard to see the bear.

TOEFL Vocabulary Practice

F. Fill in the blanks with the correct words.

attacked	opportunity	determine	surroundings	extreme

1. Many French castles have beautiful _____.

2. World War II started when Germany _____ Poland.

3. A hurricane is an example of _____ weather.

4. Poor people often do not have the _____ to travel abroad.

5. It is sometimes difficult to _____ who is right in a debate.

Practice

A. Learn the words.

Key Vocabulary

hibernate	to sleep all winter
wake up	to stop sleeping
cave	a large hole in rock or the ground

TOEFL Vocabulary

rare	unusual, not common
gather	to make or form into a group
prepare	to make or become ready
shelter	something that provides a home
protect	to make safe

B. Read the passage and underline the key information.

Hibernation

It is rare to see bats, mice, snakes, or bears in winter. This is because they hibernate. Hibernation is when an animal sleeps all winter.

When an animal hibernates, it usually goes to sleep in the fall. Then, in the spring, it wakes up. An animal will do this because there is not much food in winter. Therefore, it goes to sleep.

The animal will gather and eat a lot of food. It does this to prepare for such a long sleep. It does not eat while it is hibernating.

At the end of fall, it is usually fat. Then it goes into its warm shelter. There are many kinds of shelters. Typical ones are caves, holes, or empty trees. The shelter protects the animal from the cold.

The animal usually sleeps for five months. When it wakes up, it is hungry. So, the animal eats. Then it all starts again!

C. Choose the correct answers.

1. Which of the following best expresses the essential information in the highlighted sentence? Incorrect answers change the meaning in important ways or leave out essential information.

   When an animal hibernates, it usually goes to sleep in the fall.

   (A) Animals sleep in the summer.
   (B) Animals normally start hibernating in the fall.

2. According to the passage, animals that hibernate eat a lot of food during the summer because

   (A) they do not eat while they hibernate
   (B) it helps them sleep in the winter

3. According to the passage, which is NOT true of a hibernating animal?

   (A) It usually goes to sleep in the fall.
   (B) The animals are hungry at the end of fall.

TOEFL Vocabulary Practice

D. Fill in the blanks with the correct words.

rare	prepare	gather	shelters	protect

1. Paintings by Pablo Picasso are very _____ and expensive.

2. Every year millions of Muslims _____ in Mecca to pray.

3. You must _____ for a test if you want to pass.

4. The police _____ people from criminals.

5. Eskimos made _____ out of ice called igloos.

Read the passage.

How Animals Protect Themselves

■ **1)** Have you ever walked in the grass and smelled something terrible? The smell might be skunk spray. A skunk will spray something that attacks it. ■ **2)** It can shoot its spray very far. It makes everything smell horrible. It is hard to clean from fur. A sprayed animal will smell for weeks. A skunk will use its spray to stop from being attacked. It wants to protect its babies and shelter. So if you ever see a baby skunk, prepare to be sprayed! ■ **3)**

■ **4)** Other animals protect themselves in different ways. A buffalo is very heavy, but it still needs to be protected. It likes to be in a large group with many other buffalo. This group is called a herd. The herd protects it. A wolf will often attack a buffalo. A wolf is very strong and dangerous. The herd protects the buffalo. The herd makes it hard for a wolf to kill a buffalo. This is because the wolf has to go past all the others in the herd. Wolves are also scared of a running herd of buffalo. Buffalo are heavy and fast. A buffalo is taller than a wolf. Therefore, a wolf will be trampled by the herd.

A wolf must wait. A buffalo away from the herd is not protected. So, a wolf will sneak up on it. Then the wolf will jump on it. This is how a wolf finds its food. The buffalo will be safe if they stay together.

Choose the correct answers.

1. The word horrible in the passage is closest in meaning to
   (A) sweet   (B) sour
   (C) good   (D) bad

2. According to the passage, buffalo gather in herds because
   (A) this is how a wolf finds food
   (B) this is how buffalo find food
   (C) wolves are scared of herds
   (D) buffalo like to be alone

3. Look at the four squares (■) that indicate where the following sentence could be added to the passage.

Of course, not only skunks protect themselves.

Where would the sentences best fit?

(A) Square 1   (B) Square 2
(C) Square 3   (D) Square 4

4. Why does the author use the following sentence?

So if you ever see a baby skunk, prepare to be sprayed!

(A) The author wants the reader to be sprayed.
(B) The author is trying to protect the reader from being sprayed.
(C) The author is trying to protect the baby skunks.
(D) The author likes the skunk spray.

5. Which of the following best expresses the essential information in the highlighted sentence? Incorrect answers change the meaning in important ways or leave out essential information.

Therefore, a wolf will be trampled by the herd.

(A) The herd will step on the wolf.
(B) The wolf will kill the buffalo.
(C) The buffalo will be scared of the wolf.
(D) Buffalo are not scared of wolves.

6. **Directions:** Complete the table below about the animal characteristics discussed in the passage. Match the characteristics to the correct animal. TWO of the answer choices will not be used.

Answer choices

(A) Large animal
(B) Small animal
(C) Gather in herds
(D) Uses spray for protection
(E) Has eight legs
(F) Protects its shelter
(G) Hibernates every year

Skunks
• _____
• _____
• _____

Buffalo
• _____
• _____

Check-up

A. Choose the correct answer.

1. *A sentence simplification* question asks

   (A) what a word or phrase means

   (B) about specific details or facts that are in the passage

   (C) for a sentence that appears in the passage

   (D) for a sentence in the passages to be restated, summarized, or simplified

Key Vocabulary Practice

B. Fill in the blanks with the correct words.

hunting	caves	hibernate	wake up	blending in	fur

1. Animals that hibernate, _____ in the spring.

2. People don't _____ during winter.

3. Iguanas are very good at _____ to what is around them.

4. In France, there are drawings on the walls of _____ that are nearly 30,000 years old!

5. Cats are good at _____ mice.

6. Some people kill tigers for their beautiful _____.

[04] Physics

Getting Ready to Read

A. Learn the words.

Key Vocabulary

solid	a substance that is hard and keeps its shape, such as wood
liquid	a substance that moves and flows, such as water
gas	a substance that is not solid or liquid, such as air

TOEFL Vocabulary

physics	science that studies physical forces
energy	the amount of activity in something
electricity	a form of energy
mechanics	the study of energy and forces
measure	to find the size or amount of something

B. Learn the question types.

TOEFL Question Types

Inference

Which of the following can be inferred about X?

The author of the passage implies that X . . .

- This type of question asks what is implied, but not stated, in the passage.
- The answer will support or incorporate ideas from the passage.

Rhetorical Purpose

Why does the author mention X?

The author discusses X in order to . . .

The author uses X as an example of . . .

- This type of question asks why the author has written something in a certain way or why they have used information in a certain place.
- This type of question also often asks how a statement or paragraph relates to the rest of the passage.

C. **Read the passage. Number each paragraph with the correct main idea or purpose.**

> 1. What matter is
> 2. Example of physics
> 3. What energy is
> 4. What Physics is

Physics

___Physics is a science. It looks at energy and matter. It includes the study of light, heat, sound, electricity, and mechanics.

___Energy is the way things move and how work is done. Some things have a lot of energy. Other things do not.

___Matter is what things are made of. Solids, liquids, and gasses are all matter.

___Energy and matter are everywhere. For example, we need energy to boil water. Water is liquid matter. We add heat to the water. This heat is energy. The energy makes the water boil. The water changes into a gas called steam. Scientists can measure this energy and matter. This is an example of physics.

Note-taking

D. **Complete the summary notes by filling in the blanks.**

Topic:	Physics
Introduction:	_____ is a science.
	Looks at _____ and matter.
	Studies light, heat, sound _____, and mechanics.
Energy:	_____ is the way things move and how work is done.
	_____ things have a lot of energy. Some do not.
Matter:	Matter is what things are _____ of.
	Solids, liquids, and gasses are all _____.
Heat:	Heat is _____.
	This energy makes water _____.
	Scientists _____ energy and matter.

E. Choose the correct answers.

1. Which of the following can be inferred from paragraph 3?

  (A) Everything is made of matter.

  (B) There would not be movement without heat.

2. The author mentions science in order to

  (A) explain how physics works

  (B) explain what physics is

3. Which of the following can be inferred about heat from paragraph 4?

  (A) Heat can change a liquid into a gas.

  (B) Water is a kind of energy.

4. The author uses heat as an example of

  (A) a way we can use energy

  (B) how to measure water

TOEFL Vocabulary Practice

F. Fill in the blanks with the correct words.

electricity	mechanics	physics	energy	measure

1. We use a ruler to _____ the length of something.

2. Computers need _____ to work.

3. An engineer uses _____ to design a new machine.

4. When you study _____, you look at energy and matter.

5. You need a lot of _____, to hit a ball far.

Practice

A. Learn the words.

Key Vocabulary

kinetic	active, moving
move	to change position
pass	transfer

TOEFL Vocabulary

object	something that is not alive
destroy	ruin; damage
potential	possible; likely
transfer	move from one place to another
result	conclusion; outcome

B. Read the passage and underline the key information.

Energy

Energy is the work an object can do. Energy cannot be made. It cannot be destroyed. It is always there. There are two types of energy. Potential energy is one. Kinetic energy is the other.

A car at the top of a hill has potential energy. The car is not moving. At any time, the car could go down the hill. This is its potential energy.

If the car goes down the hill, it is moving. This movement is kinetic energy.

Energy can also pass from one thing to another. When a golfer hits a ball, energy is transferred to the ball. The golfer passes energy to the ball. The golfer can pass a little or a lot of energy to the ball. We can see the result. A ball with a lot of energy goes far. A ball with a little energy does not.

C. Choose the correct answers.

1. Which of the following can be inferred about energy?

(A) An object can change the type of energy it has.

(B) The type of energy depends on the object.

2. Why does the author mention a golfer hitting a golf ball?

(A) To give an example of how potential energy works.

(B) To give an example of how energy can be transferred.

3. Which of the following best expresses the essential information in the highlighted sentence? Incorrect answers change the meaning in important ways or leave out essential information.

A ball with a lot of energy goes far.

(A) Balls have a lot of energy.

(B) The harder you hit the ball, the farther it will go.

TOEFL Vocabulary Practice

D. Fill in the blanks with the correct words.

destroyed	potential	object	transfer	result

1. When traveling by subway, it is often necessary to _____ to another line.

2. Energy cannot be _____.

3. Adding heat to water will _____ in the water boiling.

4. A tornado has the _____ to do a lot of damage.

5. A scale is an _____ that measures weight.

Read the passage.

Thomas Edison and the Light Bulb

Thomas Edison was an inventor. An inventor is someone who is the first person to make something. Many people think that Edison invented the light bulb. However, Edison did not. He improved the light bulb.

The light bulb was invented in 1802. Sir Humphrey Davy made it. However, the first light bulb was not very good. It gave light for only a short time. It did not work well. Edison wanted to be the first to make a useful light bulb.

Many other inventors also wanted to make a good light bulb. It had the potential to be very useful. Edison had more than 3000 ideas on how to make a better light bulb. He finally found the right one. In 1879, Edison made the first useful light bulb.

Each light bulb has a small piece of wire or thread in it. This object is called the filament. Edison used a special matter on the filament. It could make the light bulb burn longer. It did not cost much. This meant that more people could use the light bulb.

People still needed energy to use the light bulbs. Edison made a special system to help. It transferred electricity from one place to another. It moved the electricity through wires to homes and businesses. This made the light bulb popular.

The light bulb is still very important. ■ **1)** People all over the world use it. ■ **2)** It changed the world. ■ **3)** Edison made light bulbs less expensive. ■ **4)** He understood physics. The result was that he became the most famous inventor of the 1900s.

Choose the correct answers.

1. The word improved in the passage is closest in meaning to
(A) made better
(B) repaired
(C) carried
(D) burned

2. According to paragraph 2, which of the following is true of Edison?
(A) He invented the first light bulb.
(B) He made the light bulb better.
(C) He developed 3000 useful inventions.
(D) He worked with many other inventors.

3. Which of the following best expresses the essential information in the highlighted sentence? Incorrect answers change the meaning in important ways or leave out essential information.

Edison wanted to be the first to make a useful light bulb.

(A) He wanted to come up with an idea for a new kind of lightning.
(B) He wanted to make a better light bulb before anyone else.
(C) He wanted to be the first to invent a light bulb that could be used.
(D) He wanted to invent a light bulb that had different uses.

4. What can be inferred about Edison's invention from paragraph 5?

(A) It wouldn't work without electricity.
(B) It was used by very few businesses.
(C) It couldn't be used in many homes.
(D) Edison's light bulb was very expensive

5. Look at the four squares (■) that indicate where the following sentence could be added to the passage.

He also made them more useful.

Where would the sentence best fit?

(A) Square 1   (B) Square 2
(C) Square 3   (D) Square 4

6. **Directions:** An introductory sentence for a brief summary of the passage is provided below. Complete the summary by selecting the THREE answer choices that express the most important ideas in the passage. Some sentences do not belong in the summary because they express ideas that are not presented in the passage or are minor ideas in the passage.

Thomas Edison changed the world.

Answer choices

(A) He made the first useful light bulb.
(B) He came up with the idea for the first light bulb.
(C) He made light bulbs cost less and burn longer.
(D) He also made electricity available to people.
(E) He discovered electricity for the first time in 1879.

Check-up

A. Choose the correct answers.

1. An inference question asks

   (A) about specific details or facts that are in the passage

   (B) what can NOT be implied from the passage

   (C) what can be implied from the passage

   (D) why the author has written something in a certain way or in a certain place

2. A rhetorical purpose question asks

   (A) why the author has written something in a certain way or in a certain place

   (B) what can be implied from the passage

   (C) why the author has NOT written something in a certain way or in a certain place

   (D) for a sentence in the passages to be restated, summarized, or simplified

Key Vocabulary Practice

B. Fill in the blanks with the correct words.

solid	moving	gas	passing	liquid	kinetic

1. Many people think gasoline is a _____, but it is actually a liquid.

2. We can boil water by _____ heat from a flame into it.

3. A _____ is a material that can keep its shape.

4. Rain falling from the sky has _____ energy.

5. Ice is a solid, but water would be an example of a _____.

6. A _____ car is an example of kinetic energy.

[05] Business

Getting Ready to Read

A. Learn the words.

Key Vocabulary

hard work	something that is not easy to do
sell	to give something to someone else for money
website	a page that people can look at on the Internet

TOEFL Vocabulary

business	something formed to do work in order to make money
detail	a small piece of information
decide	to pick one choice over another
charge	to ask for; make pay
choose	to pick

B. Learn the question type.

TOEFL Question Type

Insert Text

Look at the four squares that indicate where the following sentence could be added to the passage.

[You will see a sentence in bold.]

Where would the sentence best fit?

- This type of question asks for another sentence to be placed into the passage.
- The answer will connect logically and grammatically to the sentences on either side.

C. Read the passage. Number each paragraph with the correct main idea or purpose.

> 1. Details on choosing a name
> 2. Why you need a website
> 3. What the passage is about
> 4. Information on what you will sell

Starting a Business

___ ■ 1) Starting a business can be hard work. ■ 2) There are a lot of details to think about. ■ 3) There is a lot to do before you can start selling things. ■ 4)
___First, you need to decide what you will sell. You also need to know how much money you will charge for it. ■ 5)
___Next, you have to choose a name for your business. ■ 6) This is very important. ■ 7) It lets people know a lot about your business. ■ 8)
___After you have a name, you may want a website. It will let people all over the world find out about your business.

D. Complete the summary notes by filling in the blanks.

Topic:	Starting a Business
Introduction:	Can be hard work.
	A lot of _____.
	A lot to do before _____ things.
What to sell:	Decide what to _____.
	Decide what to _____.
Name:	_____ a name.
	• Is important
	• Lets people _____ about your business
Website:	Lets people find out about your _____.

E. Choose the correct answers.

1. Look at the four squares (■) that indicate where the following sentence could be added to the passage.

It can be much harder than most people think.

Where would the sentence best fit?

(A) Square 1   (B) Square 2
(C) Square 3   (D) Square 4

2. Look at the four squares (■) that indicate where the following sentence could be added to the passage.

It also helps people remember your business.

Where would the sentence best fit?

(A) Square 5   (B) Square 6
(C) Square 7   (D) Square 8

TOEFL Vocabulary Practice

F. Fill in the blanks with the correct words.

choose	decide	detail	charge	business

1. Many restaurants don't _____ for water.

2. When at the library, you can only _____ a few books to take home.

3. Many high school seniors have to _____ on what university to go to.

4. A new _____ often does not make much money.

5. The most successful business owners pay attention to every _____.

Practice

A. Learn the words.

Key Vocabulary

buy	to get something by giving someone else money
sign	something that has words and/or pictures on it
curious	wanting to know or try something

TOEFL Vocabulary

advertise	to use pictures and/or words to make people aware of something
goal	purpose; aim
original	new; not copied from somewhere else; being the first of something
example	a sample that represents all of a group or type
company	a business; something that does work to make money

B. Read the passage and underline the key information.

Advertising

Businesses all over the world advertise. ■ 1) The goal is to get people to buy the things they sell. ■ 2) People don't buy things just because you tell them to. ■ 3) Therefore, businesses use pictures, writing, and words. ■ 4) These are called advertisements. Often, they are called adverts or ads.

There are many different ways to advertise. Businesses put ads in newspapers. They also put them on the radio and TV. There are some ads that are very original. For example, some companies put ads on straws. Others pull long signs through the air behind airplanes.

One of the most famous ad ideas used small signs in the ground. For example, people driving down the road saw a sign. It said, "Eat." They saw another sign after they drove a little more. It said "warm." Then the last sign said "cookies." The signs made people curious.

Most companies now use ads. Some big companies spend millions of dollars on ads.

C. Choose the correct answers.

1. Look at the four squares (■) that indicate where the following sentence could be added to the passage.

Sometimes, they even use songs.

Where would the sentence best fit?

(A) Square 1   (B) Square 2
(C) Square 3   (D) Square 4

2. Which of the following can be inferred about advertising?

(A) Advertising is important to a business.
(B) Signs are the only method of advertising.

3. The author mentions newspapers, radio, and TV in order to

(A) show that there are many ways to advertise
(B) show that advertising is expensive

TOEFL Vocabulary Practice

D. Fill in the blanks with the correct words.

goal	original	company	example	advertise

1. Ford is an American car _____.

2. French is an _____ of a language.

3. The main _____ of exercise is to stay healthy.

4. It is very expensive to _____ on TV.

5. An inventor needs to come up with an _____ idea to be successful.

Read the passage.

Entrepreneurs

An entrepreneur is a person that starts a business. He or she takes many risks. He or she needs to have many abilities. Not everyone has these. However, you need them to be successful. Do you have them? There are five main things that most entrepreneurs have.

The first thing you need to be is a leader. Leaders can tell other people what to do. However, leaders also know when to listen. Leaders get things done quickly and easily. They pay attention to details.

Thinking of original ideas is also important to start a business. It can help you a lot. For example, it can help you choose what kind of business to have. It can help you decide how to run it. It can also help you advertise your business. It takes many original thoughts to come up with a good idea for a business.

■ **1)** You should be prepared to do a lot of hard work. ■ **2)** You should have big goals. ■ **3)** Most of all, you should want to be the best. ■ **4)** Do you like to be the best at what you do?

You also need to be good with money. This way, you know what to charge for the things you sell. Also, you must know how to save money.

Lastly, you need to be able to take risks. This means that you know you might fail, but you try anyway. It takes all of these things to start a business.

Choose the correct answers.

1. The word abilities is closest in meaning to

(A) problems (B) ideas
(C) skills (D) money

2. According to paragraph 2, leaders do all of the following EXCEPT

(A) tell people what needs to be done
(B) do all the work themselves
(C) listen to other people
(D) work on things quickly

3. Which of the following best expresses the essential information in the highlighted sentence? Incorrect answers change the meaning in important ways or leave out essential information.

It takes many original thoughts to come up with a good idea for a business.

(A) To get a good idea for a business you need to think.
(B) Good ideas are more important than original thoughts.
(C) The first thought is usually the best idea for a business.
(D) A good idea for a business requires many new thoughts.

4. Look at the four squares (■) that indicate where the following sentence could be added to the passage.

You should have big ideas, too.

Where would the sentence best fit?

(A) Square 1   (B) Square 2
(C) Square 3   (D) Square 4

5. What can be inferred about entrepreneurs from paragraph 5?

(A) They work a lot with banks.
(B) They have to be careful with their money.
(C) They think money should not be spent.
(D) They charge too much for the things they sell.

6. **Directions:** An introductory sentence for a brief summary of the passage is provided below. Complete the summary by selecting the THREE answer choices that express the most important ideas in the passage. Some sentences do not belong in the summary because they express ideas that are not presented in the passage or are minor ideas in the passage.

Entrepreneurs are people who start their own businesses.

Answer choices

(A) There are many abilities that they need.
(B) They take many risks to start their businesses.
(C) Sometimes entrepreneurs fail.
(D) They have their own employees.
(E) Most entrepreneurs make a lot of money.

Check-up

A. **Choose the correct answer.**

1. An *insert text* question asks

    (A) about details or facts that are NOT in the passage
    (B) for a sentence to be removed from the passage
    (C) for a sentence in the passage to be restated, summarized, or simplified
    (D) for another sentence to be placed into the passage

Key Vocabulary Practice

B. **Fill in the blanks with the correct words.**

curious	hard work	buy	sells	website	sign

1. You can advertise on the internet by starting a _____.

2. Most shops have a _____ above their door.

3. A supermarket _____ food.

4. Many people feel that _____ is the key to success.

5. Most people do not make clothes, they _____ them from a shop.

6. Many children are very _____ about everything.

[06] Astronomy

Getting Ready to Read

A. Learn the words.

Key Vocabulary

solar	having to do with the sun
inside	in something
atmosphere	outer layer of gases around a planet or star

TOEFL Vocabulary

segment	part
core	the central part of something
surface	the outer part of something
eventually	after a long time
survive	to continue to be

B. Learn the question type.

TOEFL Question Type

Summary

Directions: An introductory sentence for a brief summary of the passage is provided below. Complete the summary by selecting the THREE answer choices that express the most important ideas in the passage. Some sentences do not belong in the summary because they express ideas that are not presented in the passage or are minor ideas in the passage.

This will be a correct summary sentence written in bold.

• This type of question asks for the main ideas in the passage to be identified.
• The incorrect answer choices will state minor ideas or ideas that are not in the passage at all.

C. Read the passage. Number each paragraph with the correct main idea or purpose.

1. Information on the surface of the sun
2. What the passage is about
3. Information on the atmosphere of the sun
4. Information on the solar core
5. What will happen to the sun

The Sun

___The sun is a star. A star is a giant circle of burning gas. There are three main parts to the sun.

___The first segment of the sun is the solar core. It is deep inside the sun and is extremely hot.

___The second segment of the sun is called the photosphere. It is the surface and it is much cooler than the solar core.

___The third segment of the sun is its atmosphere, which is called the corona. We cannot see it from Earth. This is because it is not solid. It is made of different gases.

___The sun will change and eventually die. It does not have enough energy to survive forever.

Note-taking

D. Complete the summary notes by filling in the blanks.

Topic:	The sun
Introduction:	Is a _____.
	Is a _____ circle of burning _____.
	Has three main _____.
First Segment:	Solar _____
	• Deep _____
	• Extremely _____
Second Segment:	_____
	• Called photosphere
	• _____ than core
Third Segment:	Atmosphere
	• Called _____
	• Can't see it from _____
Conclusion:	Will change and _____ die.
	Does not have enough _____ to _____.

E. Choose the correct answers.

Directions: An introductory sentence for a brief summary of the passage is provided below. Complete the summary by selecting the THREE answer choices that express the most important ideas in the passage. Some sentences do not belong in the summary because they express ideas that are not presented in the passage or are minor ideas in the passage

1. The sun is a star with three main parts.

Answer Choices

(A) The surface is called the photosphere.
(B) The solar core is inside the sun.
(C) The corona is the solid part of the sun.
(D) The core is the coolest part of the sun.
(E) The sun's corona is its atmosphere.

2. The sun will not last forever.

Answer Choices

(A) The sun is made up of burning gasses.
(B) The solar core is on the surface of the sun.
(C) The sun does not have enough energy to burn forever.
(D) The sun is made up of three parts: the core, the surface, and the atmosphere.
(E) The sun's corona will last forever.

TOEFL Vocabulary Practice

F. Fill in the blanks with the correct words.

segments	core	surface	eventually	survived

1. The pyramids in Egypt have _____ for thousands of years.

2. About 71% of the Earth's _____ is covered with water.

3. The _____ of a baseball is made of cork or rubber.

4. A telescope is made of several _____ that fit together.

5. _____ people will live in space.

Practice

A. Learn the words.

Key Vocabulary

total	complete
partial	incomplete
orbit	to move in a circular path around a larger object

TOEFL Vocabulary

astronomy	the study of space
block	to hide from view
entire	whole
outline	the outer edges of something; not the middle
event	things that happen

B. Read the passage and underline the key information.

Solar Eclipses

Solar eclipses are very interesting. They are often studied in astronomy. An eclipse happens when the sun is blocked by the moon. There are two kinds of solar eclipses. The first is a total eclipse. The second is a partial eclipse.

A total eclipse is when the entire sun is blocked by the moon. Sometimes, as the moon orbits the Earth, it passes between the Earth and the sun. This makes the sun look dark. All that can be seen is an outline.

A partial eclipse is when only part of the sun can be seen. This happens when only part of the moon is between the Earth and the sun.

Most people think that an eclipse is an interesting event. However, it can be very dangerous to look at. ■ 1) The sun is very bright. ■ 2) It can damage the eyes. ■ 3) Even looking at a total eclipse is dangerous. ■ 4)

C. Choose the correct answers.

1. Look at the four squares (■) that indicate where the following sentence could be added to the passage.

That's why you need special glasses to view an eclipse.

Where would the sentence best fit?

(A) Square 1   (B) Square 2

(C) Square 3   (D) Square 4

2. Directions: An introductory sentence for a brief summary of the passage is provided below. Complete the summary by selecting the THREE answer choices that express the most important ideas in the passage. Some sentences do not belong in the summary because they express ideas that are not presented in the passage or are minor ideas in the passage.

A solar eclipse occurs when the moon passes between the Earth and the sun.

Answer Choices

(A) Eclipses are very common.

(B) A partial eclipse only blocks part of the sun.

(C) A total eclipse occurs when the moon blocks the entire sun.

(D) Partial eclipses look like a shadow on the surface of the sun.

(E) Eclipses can cause eye damage if looked at.

D. Fill in the blanks with the correct words.

blocked	events	astronomy	entire	outline

1. Some weather _____, such as strong tornados, can be very dangerous.

2. When drawing a person, most people start with an _____.

3. _____ is the study of the stars, planets, and universe.

4. From space, astronauts can take pictures of the _____ Earth.

5. When there are many clouds, the view of the sun is _____.

Read the passage.

Meteors

Meteors are pieces of rock in space. They float through space in groups. These groups are called meteor streams. Eventually, they enter Earth's atmosphere. This causes a special event. In astronomy, it is known as a meteor shower.

Meteor showers happen a lot. The Earth orbits the sun. As it does, it runs into many meteor streams. Scientists have found many of these meteor streams. They know of thirteen big streams that cause showers. Every year the Earth passes through the same meteor streams. Therefore, scientists can guess when the next one will happen. They know that meteor showers will happen each year at the same time. Sometimes many meteors enter the Earth's atmosphere at the same time. This is called a meteor storm.

■ 1) Meteors enter the Earth's atmosphere at high speeds. ■ 2) Meteors are usually small. ■ 3) Because they are so small, many of them burn up before they enter the atmosphere. ■ 4) The burning meteors make trails of fire. These can be seen from Earth. Many people call these falling stars. Very few ever make it inside the Earth's atmosphere.

Sometimes, a few meteors do make it through the atmosphere. When they do, they are called meteorites. However, the entire meteor will not survive. Only the segment that was not burnt when it entered the atmosphere will survive. When these hit the surface of the Earth, they can start fires or hit things, like cars.

Choose the correct answers.

1. The word orbits in the passage means
   - (A) blocks the light
   - (B) passes up
   - (C) moves away from
   - (D) goes around

2. According to paragraph 2, all of the following are true EXCEPT
   - (A) there are very few known meteor streams
   - (B) Earth passes through the same streams each year
   - (C) scientists can predict when meteor showers will occur
   - (D) a meteor storm involves more meteors than a meteor shower

3. Which of the following best expresses the essential information in the highlighted sentence? Incorrect answers change the meaning in important ways or leave out essential information.

Every year, the Earth passes through the same meteor streams.

(A) All the meteor streams that Earth passes through are similar.
(B) The meteor streams pass through Earth's atmosphere the same year.
(C) All the meteors in the streams are passed through Earth's atmosphere.
(D) The same meteor streams are passed through by Earth every year.

4. Look at the four squares (■) that indicate where the following sentence could be added to the passage.

In fact, they can be as small as a grain of sand.

Where would the sentence best fit?

(A) Square 1
(B) Square 2
(C) Square 3
(D) Square 4

5. Which of the following can be inferred about meteorites from paragraph 4?

(A) Many meteors hit the Earth everyday.
(B) It is not common for meteorites to hit the Earth.
(C) There are many more meteors than meteorites.
(D) Meteorites are very big.

6. Directions: An introductory sentence for a brief summary of the passage is provided below. Complete the summary by selecting the THREE answer choices that express the most important ideas in the passage. Some sentences do not belong in the summary because they express ideas that are not presented in the passage or are minor ideas in the passage.

Meteor showers are meteors entering the Earth's atmosphere.

Answer Choices

(A) Meteor showers are caused by meteor streams.
(B) Meteors are different from falling stars.
(C) Meteors are the size of a grain of sand.
(D) Meteors usually burn up when they hit the atmosphere.
(E) Meteor showers can cause some damage to Earth's surface.

Check-up

A. Choose the correct answer.

1. A summary question asks

   (A) for another sentence to be placed into the passage
   (B) about details or facts that are in the passage
   (C) for the main ideas in the passage to be identified
   (D) what a word or phrase refers to

Key Vocabulary Practice

B. Fill in the blanks with the correct words.

solar	inside	total	partial	orbit	atmosphere

1. The oxygen in Earth's _____ allows living things to breathe.

2. Many people get electricity for their home from _____ panels that are put on their roofs.

3. The Earth's _____ takes it through several meteor streams each year.

4. A _____ solar eclipse blocks only a portion of the sun.

5. It is very hot _____ the Earth's core.

6. Even a _____ eclipse can be dangerous to look at.

[Review 1]

Read the passage.

Benetton

Benetton is a company that makes clothes. A brother and a sister started it. They were poor. The sister made clothes for another company. However, she didn't like the clothes. They were dull. Therefore, in her free time, she made bright clothes. Her brother was a salesman. He sold clothes. He liked his sister's style. In 1955 they decided to start a business. Benetton would eventually become very well known. It is one of the most famous stores in the clothing industry.

Now Benetton is best known for its style of advertising. Most ads use the thing being sold. Other ads show beautiful, happy people using the thing being sold. However, Benetton chooses not to do that. Although Benetton makes clothes, they often use pictures that don't show any clothes. They also often use pictures that get people's attention. Benetton say that they want to make people think. ■ **1)** For example, one ad shows people of different races posing together. ■ **2)** Another shows a newborn baby. The baby has not yet been cleaned. ■ **3)**

The goal is to sell many clothes. ■ **4)** However, Benetton had an odd way of doing it. Some people did not like that way of advertising. They wanted to destroy the company. However, it has survived. Their customers like the original style of advertising.

Choose the correct answers.

1. Which of the following can be inferred about the sister?

(A) She hated making clothes.

(B) She was happier making clothes for Benetton.

(C) She didn't like her brother.

(D) She couldn't make very good clothes.

2. Which of the following best expresses the essential information in the highlighted sentence? Incorrect answers change the meaning in important ways or leave out essential information.

Benetton is best known for its style of advertising.

(A) Benetton advertisements are famous.
(B) People only know Benetton because of their advertising.
(C) Benetton has the best advertisements.
(D) Benetton's style of clothes are well-known.

3. The word posing in the passage is closest in meaning to

(A) standing   (B) running
(C) eating   (D) mailing

4. According to the passage, which is NOT true of Benetton?

(A) It is most well-known for its ads.
(B) One of their ads shows a newborn baby.
(C) It has an odd style of ads.
(D) Everybody loved its ads.

5. According to the passage, some people wanted to destroy Benetton because they didn't like

(A) the clothes   (B) the advertisements
(C) babies   (D) the sister

6. Look at the four squares (■) that indicate where the following sentence could be added to the passage.

It is also crying.

Where would the sentence best fit?

(A) Square 1   (B) Square 2
(C) Square 3   (D) Square 4

Read the passage.

First Moon Landing

Going to the moon is not easy. To get there you have to reach extreme speeds. You don't want to get pulled back by Earth's gravity. That's the thing that keeps you on the ground. When you reach the moon, you have to slow down. That's because the moon has gravity too. You have to determine just the right speed. Space travel is very dangerous. Therefore, you have to protect the people on board. You cannot make any mistakes. You have to measure the speed carefully.

The leader of the US first introduced the idea of going to the moon in 1961. However, the first moon landing wasn't until 1969. It was an important event. Neil Armstrong was the first person to walk on the surface of the moon. He and his crew gathered information for two and a half hours. They took pictures and wrote down details about what they saw. They also took pieces from the core of the moon.

Going to space is bad for the body. It is not normal, so the body finds it difficult. Still, it was a rare opportunity for the people who went. They inspired many young people to study astronomy. This is the branch of physics that deals with space. They also inspired people to study mechanics. These people wanted to build the next space rocket and go into space.

Choose the correct answers.

1. According to the passage, which of the following is NOT true of going to the moon?
   (A) You have to be careful of the speed.
   (B) It is very dangerous.
   (C) You have to be careful of the gravity.
   (D) It is easy to get there.

2. Why does the author mention gravity?
   (A) To explain how to walk on the moon
   (B) To explain why you should study mechanics
   (C) To explain why you have to go fast
   (D) To explain why no one went to the moon until 1969

3. The word he in the passage refers to

(A) the leader of the US   (B) Neil Armstrong
(C) the crew   (D) young people

4. The author of the passage implies that

(A) the crew went too fast
(B) the leader of the US and Neil Armstrong were friends
(C) not many people went to the moon
(D) Neil Armstrong was the last person to go to the moon

5. Directions: An introductory sentence for a brief summary of the passage is provided below. Complete the summary by selecting the THREE answer choices that express the most important ideas in the passage. Some sentences do not belong in the summary because they express ideas that are not presented in the passage or are minor ideas in the passage.

Neil Armstrong was the first person to go to the moon.

Answer Choices

(A) It's important to be careful of speed and gravity when going to the moon.
(B) The leader of the US thought about going to the moon.
(C) Going to the moon for the first time was important.
(D) After the first moon trip, many other people wanted to go there.
(E) Many people have been to the moon.

Reading 3

Read the passage.

The Iron Curtain

The Iron Curtain was not a real object. It was an imaginary line. It showed how Europe was divided. It was divided into the East and the West. This was after World War II. The leader of Great Britain thought of the name. The East consisted of communist nations. This is when the government owns all the resources. They traded amongst themselves. They did not allow people to leave. The West consisted of capitalist nations. This is when people and companies own most of the resources.

Some places were split in half. Berlin is a city in Germany. The entire city was divided. ■ 1) Half of the city was capitalist. ■ 2) The other half was communist. ■ 3) The communist section wanted to prevent people from leaving. ■ 4) Therefore, a wall was built through the middle of the city. If anyone tried to cross, they were killed.

This was all part of the Cold War. On one side were capitalist nations. On the other side were communist ones. It lasted nearly half a century. Each side was afraid of the other. They developed dangerous weapons called nuclear weapons. These had the potential to destroy many things. This had an important impact on the relationship between the nations. However, no one used their nuclear weapons. Finally, the Cold War ended. Many people came to the conclusion that communism wasn't working. The Berlin Wall came down. This was an important event. The result was that the West won.

Choose the correct answers.

1. The word It in the passage refers to
   (A) Europe
   (C) The Iron Curtain
   (B) Berlin
   (D) World War II

2. The word prevent in the passage is closest in meaning to
   (A) split
   (C) stop
   (B) kill
   (D) allow

3. The author's description of the Iron Curtain mentions which of the following?

(A) It was a real object.

(B) It took a long time to build.

(C) It divided America.

(D) It was an imaginary line.

4. Look at the four squares (■) that indicate where the following sentence could be added to the passage.

They also wanted to stop information from being transferred in.

Where would the sentence best fit?

(A) Square 1

(B) Square 2

(C) Square 3

(D) Square 4

5. Which of the following best expresses the essential information in the highlighted sentence? Incorrect answers change the meaning in important ways or leave out essential information.

These had the potential to destroy many things.

(A) They were very safe to use.

(B) They could have damaged many things.

(C) They were used many times.

(D) They were unlikely to damage anything.

6. The author uses Berlin as an example of

(A) an area that used nuclear weapons

(B) how places were split between East and West

(C) a capitalist nation

(D) how communists won the Cold War

[07] Literature

Getting Ready to Read

A. Learn the words.

Key Vocabulary

print	to put words on to paper using a machine
copy	one of a number of books, newspaper, etc. that have been printed at the same time
list	a group of things arranged in a certain way

TOEFL Vocabulary

popular	well-liked
organize	to arrange
describe	to tell about
struggle	to fight
character	a person in a book or movie

B. Learn the question types.

TOEFL Question Types

Vocabulary

The word X in the passage is closest in meaning to . . .

In stating X, the author means that . . .

- This type of question asks for the meaning of a word or phrase in the context of how it is used in the passage.
- It is usually a word that is important to understanding part of the passage.

Reference

The word X in the passage refers to . . .

- This type of question asks for what a word or phrase is referring to.
- The word is often a pronoun.

C. Read the passage. Number each paragraph with the correct main idea or purpose.

> 1. Details on a famous bestseller
> 2. What the passage is about
> 3. Describes bestseller lists
> 4. Information on number of copies of bestsellers

Bestsellers

___Every year, many books are printed. However, few become popular. When a book sells many copies, it is called a bestseller.

___There are many bestseller lists. This is when books are organized by how many they have sold. The book that sells the most is first on the list.

___There are many bestsellers. Some of the most famous are the Harry Potter books. These books describe a boy's struggle against bad people. This has made the Harry Potter character very well known.

___Bestsellers sell a lot more copies than most books do. For example, one Harry Potter book has sold 107 million copies. It is one of the most popular books ever.

D. Complete the summary notes by filling in the blanks.

Topic: Bestsellers

Introduction: Many books are _____ but only a few become _____.

Bestsellers are _____ that sell a lot of _____.

Bestseller Lists: _____ by how many sold.

Sell the most = first on list.

Bestseller: Harry Potter is one of most _____ bestsellers.

- A boy's _____ against bad people
- _____ very well known

Copies: Sell more than most books.

Harry Potter sold _____ million.

- One of the most _____ ever

E. Choose the correct answers.

1. The word few in the passage is closest in meaning to

(A) a lot   (B) not many

2. The phrase these books in the passage refers to

(A) bestsellers   (B) the Harry Potter books

3. The word copies in the passage is closest in meaning to

(A) a number of books   (B) a number of customers

4. The word it in the passage refers to

(A) a Harry Potter book   (B) people

TOEFL Vocabulary Practice

F. Fill in the blanks with the correct words.

characters	popular	organized	struggles	described

1. Animals are _____ according to the species they belong to.

2. The four _____ in the book *Little Women* are Meg, Jo, Beth, and Amy.

3. A baby bird often _____ to break out of its shell.

4. Justin Timberlake is a very _____ American singer.

5. The writer Pliny the Younger _____ a famous volcano.

Practice

A. Learn the words.

Key Vocabulary

successful	having done something well; having become important, famous, or rich
trial	a meeting at a court that decides if someone is guilty of a crime
suspect	someone that the police think did a crime

TOEFL Vocabulary

publish	to print something that can be sold to people
issue	a point that many people think is important
treat	to act or behave in a particular way
crime	an action that breaks a country's law
literature	writing that is valued because of its excellence

B. Read the passage and underline the key information.

Harper Lee

Harper Lee wrote a very famous book called *To Kill a Mockingbird*. She became very well known because of her book. Of course, she worked very hard to become so successful.

Harper Lee worked on *To Kill a Mockingbird* for more than three years. It is the only book she published. She rewrote it many times. She wanted to make it very good.

Eventually, her book was published in 1960. The book looks at important issues. It deals mainly with how people treat each other. It is about the trial of a man who was a suspect in a very bad crime. He did not get a fair trial.

The book was very successful. It sold more than fifteen million copies. Harper Lee also won many important awards. In fact, she won the Pulitzer Prize. It is the highest award in literature. Many people still read her book today.

C. Choose the correct answers.

1. The word it in the passage refers to

(A) the trial   (B) the book

2. The word published in the passage is closest in meaning to

(A) printed   (B) bought

3. **Directions:** An introductory sentence for a brief summary of the passage is provided below. Complete the summary by selecting the THREE answer choices that express the most important ideas in the passage. Some sentences do not belong in the summary because they express ideas that are not presented in the passage or are minor ideas in the passage.

To Kill a Mockingbird is a very famous book.

Answer Choices

(A) It was written by Harper Lee.
(B) This book is studied in many schools.
(C) It took her three years to write.
(D) She won the Pulitzer Prize for it.
(E) The story takes place in the American South.

TOEFL Vocabulary Practice

D. Fill in the blanks with the correct words.

literature	published	treated	crimes	issue

1. Romantic _____ was written between 1815 and 1848.

2. A police officer's job is to stop people from doing _____.

3. Dangerous animals should be _____ with caution.

4. It is difficult for a writer to get his or her first book _____.

5. These days, global warming is a very important _____.

Read the passage.

Sherlock Holmes

Detective books are very popular. In these books, a detective solves a crime. There are often a lot of suspects. However, only one person is the criminal. The detective has to catch the criminal. He or she tries to find clues. The clues help the detective catch the criminal. One of the most well-known detectives in literature is Sherlock Holmes.

Most detective books have a main character like Holmes. The story usually develops around this person. This is because he or she is interesting. ■ **1)** Holmes knows how criminals think. ■ **2)** He is very good at catching them. ■ **3)** He does this by looking at clues. ■ **4)** A lot of the main characters in detective books are like Holmes.

Also, most detective books have a surprise at the end. The Sherlock Holmes books always surprise readers. Many readers like to guess the end to a story. It makes them feel smart. However, most readers struggle with the Sherlock Holmes stories. They guess the wrong suspect. Sherlock Holmes is the only one who can figure out the crime each time. He is very smart. This is what makes these books so famous.

Other detective books also use surprise endings. However, the Holmes books were first. They were first published in 1887. This is why many people think that these books are the best. They are old, but they are still interesting.

Choose the correct answers.

1. Which of the following is NOT true of detective fiction?

(A) There is more than one suspect in the crime.
(B) The detective discovers important information.
(C) There are multiple people who did the crime.
(D) The detective finds out who is guilty of the crime.

2. The word develops in the passage is closest in meaning to

(A) ends   (B) looks
(C) grows   (D) sells

3. Look at the four squares (■) that indicate where the following sentence could be added to the passage.

Then he decides who did the crime.

Where would the sentence best fit?

(A) Square 1   (B) Square 2
(C) Square 3   (D) Square 4

4. Which of the following best expresses the essential information in the highlighted sentence? Incorrect answers change the meaning in important ways or leave out essential information.

Sherlock Holmes is the only one who can figure out the crime each time.

(A) Only Sherlock Holmes knows who did the crime every time.
(B) The criminal was the only one who knew who Sherlock Holmes was.
(C) The person who committed the crime knew Sherlock Holmes.
(D) Sherlock Holmes committed the crime each time.

5. Which of the following can be inferred about the Sherlock Holmes books?
(A) The Sherlock Holmes stories influenced many detective fiction books.
(B) The surprise ending surprised even the detectives in the books.
(C) Most people were not impressed by the use of surprise endings.
(D) Detective fiction was later very different from the Sherlock Holmes books.

6. Directions: An introductory sentence for a brief summary of the passage is provided below. Complete the summary by selecting the THREE answer choices that express the most important ideas in the passage. Some sentences do not belong in the summary because they express ideas that are not presented in the passage or are minor ideas in the passage.

Detective fiction is a certain type of story.

Answer choices

(A) It involves crimes that are solved by detectives.
(B) All detective books have Sherlock Holmes in them.
(C) Sherlock Holmes books are still interesting.
(D) The most famous detective is Sherlock Holmes.
(E) Sherlock Holmes books are thought to be the best detective books because the endings are surprising.

Check-up

A. Choose the correct answers.

1. A *vocabulary* question asks

   (A) about details or facts are in the passage
   (B) for a sentence in the passage to be restated, summarized, or simplified
   (C) what a word or phrase refers to
   (D) what a word or phrase means

2. A *reference* questions asks

   (A) for the main ideas in the passage to be identified
   (B) what a word or phrase refers to
   (C) what can be implied from the passage
   (D) what a word or phrase means

Key Vocabulary Practice

B. Fill in the blanks with the correct words.

successful	trial	suspect	print	list	copy

1. When the police catch a _____, they usually take him or her to jail.

2. The outcome of a _____ is decided by a jury.

3. Most people only buy one _____ of a book.

4. Bill Gates is a very _____ businessman.

5. People who have a computer and a printer can _____ their own files.

6. Most books never get on a bestseller _____.

[08] Environment

Getting Ready to Read

A. Learn the words.

Key Vocabulary

ocean	a large body of salt water
tool	a thing that is usually held in the hand and used to do work or make something
harpoon	a long, pointed piece of metal used for catching or killing whales

TOEFL Vocabulary

efficiently	able to function without waste
planet	the Earth
international	involving many countries
law	a rule usually for a country
ban	to not allow

B. Learn the question types.

TOEFL Question Types

Factual Information

According to the author, X did Y because . . .

According to the passage, X occurred because . . .

The author's description of X mentions which of the following?

- This type of question asks about specific facts or details.
- The answer is always directly stated somewhere in the passage.

Negative Factual Information

According to the passage, which of the following is NOT true of X?

The author's description of X mentions all of the following EXCEPT . . .

- This type of question asks which fact or detail does NOT appear in the passage or is NOT correct.
- The other answer choices are usually directly stated somewhere in the passage.

C. **Read the passage. Number each paragraph with the correct main idea or purpose.**

> 1. How whales were killed.
> 2. Why whales were killed.
> 3. Introduction to humpback whales.
> 4. What people did to help whales.
> 5. What happened to the whales.

Whaling

___Humpback whales are one of the ocean's most beautiful animals. However, most of them were killed.

___For many years, people hunted whales. They hunted them for food, tools, and clothes.

___In the late 1800s a new harpoon was made. It killed whales more efficiently.

___The result was that people started to hunt a lot more whales. By 1966, 90% of the planet's humpback whales were dead.

___In 1966, an international law was made. It banned the hunting of whales. This helped to save the whales. However, some people still try to hunt whales even though there is a ban.

D. **Complete the summary notes by filling in the blanks.**

Topic:	Whaling
Introduction:	Humpback whales — _____ of oceans most beautiful _____.
	Most were _____.
Whale hunting:	Whales hunted for _____, tools, and _____.
Effects of Harpoon:	In late _____, new _____ was made.
	• Killed whales more _____
	People hunted a lot more whales.
	By 1966, _____ of _____ humpback whales dead.
Whaling laws:	_____ law banned the hunting of whales.
	Some people still try to _____ whales.

E. Choose the correct answers.

1. According to the passage, which of the following is NOT true about humpback whales?

(A) Almost all of them were killed.

(B) They are the ocean's ugliest animals.

2. According to the passage, which of the following is true about the new harpoon?

(A) It was invented in the 1900s.

(B) It killed whales more efficiently.

3. According to the passage, people hunted whales

(A) for food, tools, and clothes.

(B) to perform a show.

4. According to the passage, an international law was made to

(A) stop the hunting of whales

(B) make the harpoon illegal

TOEFL Vocabulary Practice

F. Fill in the blanks with the correct words.

efficiently	law	planet	international	banned

1. In many restaurants, smoking is _____.

2. Most of the _____ is covered by water.

3. In Italy, there is a _____ that says that a man may go to jail for wearing a skirt.

4. The United Nations is an _____ group that works to solve the world's problems.

5. Computers let us _____ get information from anywhere.

Practice

A. Learn the words.

Key Vocabulary

garbage	waste; useless material
gasoline	liquid fuel used to make cars go
smoke	a cloud of tiny particles usually caused by the burning of fuel

TOEFL Vocabulary

fuel	source of energy
discover	to find out
pollution	something that makes the area around it dirty or unclean
advantageous	useful
decrease	to go down in size or amount

B. Read the passage and underline the key information.

New Garbage Trucks

Think of a car that uses last night's dinner as fuel. Scientists in America have discovered a way to do this! They have made garbage trucks that run on garbage. Now garbage trucks do not have to use gasoline.

The trucks can do this by catching bad smelling gasses. They catch these gasses from the old garbage. They then use it as fuel. Garbage trucks use a lot of fuel. However, gasoline is expensive and dirty. It also makes a lot of pollution. There is already a lot of garbage, so it is cheap!

These new trucks are advantageous for many reasons. The new trucks are cheaper to run. They are able to use the garbage for fuel. They also help to decrease the amount of garbage that is thrown away. This helps to save land. Also, these trucks help the Earth. They do this because they do not make as much smoke. This means there is much less pollution.

C. Choose the correct answers.

1. The word discovered in the passage is closest in meaning to

(A) forgot   (B) found

2. According to the passage, garbage trucks

(A) are noisy   (B) use a lot of fuel

3. The word they in the passage refers to

(A) the new trucks   (B) the old trucks

4. According to the passage, which of the following is NOT true about the new trucks?

(A) They are more expensive to run.

(B) They can use garbage for fuel.

TOEFL Vocabulary Practice

D. Fill in the blanks with the correct words.

fuel	advantageous	pollution	decrease	discovered

1. Smoke from cars makes a lot of _____.

2. We can help to _____ the amount of trash by reusing our bags from the supermarket.

3. Cars sometimes stop running because they run out of _____.

4. Many people say that Christopher Columbus _____ America in 1492.

5. It is _____ to walk to places because it is good exercise.

Read the passage.

Cities That Help the Planet

There are ways to keep the planet clean. There are also ways to decrease pollution. Many cities in the world do things to help. In Singapore, they discovered a way to catch a lot of rain. Now they don't need to use water from rivers. The water is dirty. It is also expensive to clean. The machines that clean water also give out pollution.

San Francisco helps too. It made a law that banned plastic bags at the supermarket. This means there is a lot less trash.

Chicago also helps. New buildings must have trees and grass on their roofs. This is advantageous because it keeps buildings warm in the winter. ■ **1)** It also keeps them cool in the summer. This means less energy is used to heat or cool the buildings. ■ **2)** Plants are also very good for the air.

Many cities in Germany use wind for energy. ■ **3)** Wind is useful because it does not make smoke. This means less pollution. Wind is also free. ■ **4)**

Cities like Seoul help by having very good subways. They also have many buses. People can efficiently get around the city. This means fewer people use cars. Therefore, less gasoline or other fuels are used. This helps to decrease pollution.

Cities all over the world do things to make the planet cleaner. Some places do big things like building subways. Other cities do small things like banning plastic bags. Whatever a city does, it is good to help keep the planet clean.

Choose the correct answers.

1. The word planet in the passages is closest in meaning to

(A) pollution   (B) meteor

(C) Earth   (D) comet

2. Which of the following can be inferred about Singapore's water?

(A) They need clean water.

(B) They want to give water to other countries.

(C) They have a lot of it.

(D) They do not want a lot of it.

3. According to the passage, all of the following are being done to help clean the planet EXCEPT

(A) catching rainwater
(B) using wind
(C) taking the subway
(D) using airplanes

4. Which of the following best expresses the essential information in the highlighted sentence? Incorrect answers change the meaning in important ways or leave out essential information.

This is advantageous because it keeps buildings warm in the winter.

(A) Grass, on the roof, helps to keep heat inside the building.
(B) Catching rain makes the building warm.
(C) People are warm because they can relax.
(D) Grass makes the trees warm in the winter.

5. Look at the four squares (■) that indicate where the following sentence could be added to the passage.

Germany has a lot of wind because it is next to the sea.

Where would the sentence best fit?

(A) Square 1
(B) Square 2
(C) Square 3
(D) Square 4

6. **Directions:** An introductory sentence for a brief summary of the passage is provided below. Complete the summary by selecting the THREE answer choices that express the most important ideas in the passage. Some sentences do not belong in the summary because they express ideas that are not presented in the passage or are minor ideas in the passage.

Different cities around the world do different things to help keep the planet clean and decrease pollution.

Answer choices

(A) Chicago likes grass and trees.
(B) Singapore catches rain water, San Francisco banned plastic bags, and cities in Germany use wind power.
(C) New buildings in Chicago have grass and trees on their roofs and Seoul has a subway system.
(D) Everything a city does to avoid creating pollution is good.
(E) San Francisco only wants to help by banning plastic bags.

Check-up

A. Choose the correct answers.

1. *A factual information* question asks
   (A) what can be implied from the passage
   (B) what a word or phrase means
   (C) about details or facts that are in the passage
   (D) about details or facts that are NOT in the passage

2. *A negative factual information* question asks
   (A) about details or facts that are NOT in the passage
   (B) what a word or phrase means
   (C) for main ideas in the passage to be identified
   (D) about details or facts that are in the passage

Key Vocabulary Practice

B. Fill in the blanks with the correct words.

oceans	tools	harpoon	garbage	gasoline	smoke

1. It is not good for the environment if _____ comes out of your car.

2. Hammers, screw drivers, shovels, and drills are all examples of _____.

3. A large truck uses a lot more _____ than a small car.

4. The Atlantic and the Pacific are the two largest _____ in the world.

5. The steel _____ made it easier to kill whales.

6. We all must try to reduce the amount of _____ that we make.

[09] Health

Getting Ready to Read

A. Learn the words.

Key Vocabulary

mind	the part of a person that thinks and feels emotions
lean	not fat; slim
brain	the part of the body inside the head that controls the body's actions and processes and, in humans, the thoughts and feelings

TOEFL Vocabulary

health	the body's condition
effect	a change caused by something else; a result
chemical	a substance that causes change in something else
encourage	to suggest
reward	a good thing that happens after doing something

B. Learn the question type.

TOEFL Question Type

Sentence Simplification

Which of the following best expresses the essential information in the highlighted sentence? Incorrect answers change the meaning in important ways or leave out essential information.

- This type of question asks for the answer that best restates, summarizes, or simplifies a sentence from the passage.
- The answer will use different vocabulary or grammar and it will often use synonyms.

C. Read the passage. Number each paragraph with the correct main idea or purpose.

> 1. Exercise and the mind
> 2. How often to exercise
> 3. Exercise and the body
> 4. Exercise is great

Exercise

___Exercise is great for the body. It's great for the mind too. Some people do not like to exercise. However, those who exercise feel good in many ways.

___First, exercise makes muscles strong. It keeps the body lean. It makes the heart healthy too. A strong heart is an important effect of exercise.

___Next, exercise helps the brain make chemicals. These chemicals make people feel happy. People who are sad or angry feel better when they exercise.

___Doctors encourage people to exercise three times a week. This can be hard work. Still, the rewards from exercising are great. The body needs exercise. The mind does too.

D. Complete the summary notes by filling in the blanks.

Topic:	Exercise
Introduction:	Is great for the _____ and _____.
	Some do not like to exercise.
	Those who exercise feel _____.
Body:	Makes _____ strong, keeps body lean, makes heart _____.
	Strong heart is an important _____ of exercise.
Mind:	Helps the _____ make _____.
	• Makes people feel _____
	Sad or angry people feel _____ when they exercise.
How often:	Doctors _____ people to exercise _____ times a week.
	• Can be _____
	• _____ are great
	The body and _____ need exercise.

E. Choose the correct answers.

1. Which of the following best expresses the essential information in the highlighted sentence? Incorrect answers change the meaning in important ways or leave out essential information.

> However, those who exercise feel good in many ways.

(A) People who exercise do many different exercises.
(B) There are many good effects from exercise.

2. Which of the following best expresses the essential information in the highlighted sentence? Incorrect answers change the meaning in important ways or leave out essential information.

> A strong heart is an important effect of exercise.

(A) Making the heart stronger is one of the main benefits of exercise.
(B) Exercises for the heart are the best type of exercise.

TOEFL Vocabulary Practice

F. Fill in the blanks with the correct words.

reward	health	encourage	chemical	effect

1. Dopamine is the name of one brain _____ that makes people feel happy.

2. Not getting enough sleep can have a poor _____ on one's health.

3. A teacher should _____ his or her students to study before tests.

4. Eating right, exercising regularly, and getting plenty of rest are all necessary for good _____.

5. Feeling great is _____ for exercising regularly.

Practice

A. Learn the words.

Key Vocabulary

insect	a small six-legged animal
germ	a small organism that can make people ill
protein	plant or animal tissue that, when eaten, helps the body grow

TOEFL Vocabulary

society	a group of people living together
for instance	for example
prefer	to like better
vitamin	substances found in natural foods that help the body stay healthy
refuse	to not accept something offered

B. Read the passage and underline the key information.

Eating Insects

People in many societies eat insects. However, people in America do not like to eat them. They think that insects are dirty. They also think they have many germs. Eating insects can be healthy, though. For instance, crickets are a healthy food.

Many people in the US prefer to eat meat. They eat beef, chicken, or pork. Crickets are healthier than these meats. They have very little fat. They are high in protein. Crickets also have many vitamins.

Crickets are easy to cook. Sometimes, they are covered in chocolate. Then they are eaten as candy. Sometimes they are fried. Then they are eaten as a snack. They can be put in any food. They are even put in cookies. Crickets give food more protein.

Crickets are crunchy. They taste like nuts. A lot of people in America would refuse to eat crickets. However, there are many reasons to try these insects.

C. Choose the correct answers.

1. Which of the following best expresses the essential information in the highlighted sentence? Incorrect answers change the meaning in important ways or leave out essential information.

   People in many societies eat insects.

   (A) It is normal to eat bugs in many countries.
   (B) The custom of eating bugs is not understood by many.

2. According to the passage, crickets are a healthy food because

   (A) many people like to eat crickets
   (B) they have little fat and a lot of protein

3. According to the passage, which of the following is NOT true of crickets?

   (A) They are high in protein.   (B) They taste like meat.

D. Fill in the blanks with the correct words.

refuse	society	prefer	for instance	vitamin

1. It is impolite to _____ a drink when visiting a friend.

2. Many people _____ eating foods they are familiar with.

3. _____ C can be found in many different fruits such as oranges.

4. A _____ is a group of individuals who live together.

5. Crickets can be eaten in many ways. _____, they can be covered in chocolate and eaten as candy.

Read the passage.

How Germs Are Spread

Germs can cause many kinds of illnesses. They cannot be seen with the eye. However, they are everywhere. They are easily spread through societies in many ways. Not all germs are dangerous, but some can kill.

Germs are often spread through little liquid drops. These little drops land on people when others cough or sneeze. Sometimes, they get into another person's nose, mouth, or eyes. This can make a healthy person ill.

Another way germs are spread is through the air. Some germs refuse to die quickly. They can live in the air for a long time. If a healthy person breathes in these germs, they may become ill. These germs often have bad effects on people's breathing.

Germs that can make people ill can also be found in water. Germs can be spread through food too. These germs can even be in meat and vegetables. These types of germs in food and water can have serious effects.

Other times germs are spread through insects. Insects can have germs on or in their bodies. Sometimes these insects will bite or sting a person. This can make the person ill.

Doctors encourage people to do many things to stop spreading germs. For instance, washing hands often is important. Everyone should cover their mouths when they cough or sneeze. ■ 1) Foods should be cooked carefully. ■ 2) Also, people should stay home when they feel ill. ■ 3) These things can help germs from spreading. ■ 4)

Choose the correct answers.

1. Which of the following can be inferred about germs in food and water?

(A) It can affect large groups of people.
(B) It cannot be seen in drops.
(C) It can be treated with medicine.
(D) It can kill other germs in the water.

2. According to the passage, all of the following are true about spreading germs EXCEPT

(A) covering the mouth helps stop germs from spreading
(B) sick people should stay home and not spread their germs
(C) people should wash their hands many times a day
(D) food should be eaten quickly after it has been purchased

3. The word serious is closest in meaning to

(A) dangerous
(B) unhealthy
(C) small
(D) strange

4. Which of the following best expresses the essential information in the highlighted sentence? Incorrect answers change the meaning in important ways or leave out essential information.

Germs are often spread through little liquid drops.

(A) Little germs are spread in drops.
(B) Germs are spread mainly by liquid drops.
(C) Many people get sick from germs in little drops.
(D) Little drops have the most germs.

5. Look at the four squares (■) that indicate where the following sentence could be added to the passage.

When people are sick, they can easily make others sick.

Where would the sentence best fit?

(A) Square 1
(B) Square 2
(C) Square 3
(D) Square 4

6. Directions: An introductory sentence for a brief summary of the passage is provided below. Complete the summary by selecting the THREE answer choices that express the most important ideas in the passage. Some sentences do not belong in the summary because they express ideas that are not presented in the passage or are minor ideas in the passage.

Germs are spread in many different ways.

Answer choices

(A) Germs are commonly spread by coughing and sneezing.
(B) Food should be cooked carefully.
(C) Germs can be spread though air, food, and water.
(D) Germs can also be spread by insects.
(E) They cannot be seen with the eye.

Check-up

A. Choose the correct answer.

1. A *sentence simplification* question asks

   (A) for another sentence to be placed into the passage

   (B) for the main ideas in the passage to be identified

   (C) for a sentence in the passage to be restated, summarized, or simplified

   (D) for the main ideas in the passage to be identified

Key Vocabulary Practice

B. Fill in the blanks with the correct words.

mind	lean	brain	insect	germs	protein

1. The _____ is one of the most important organs in our body.

2. Learning a new language is one way to keep the _____ strong.

3. Exercise combined with a proper diet helps keep the body looking _____.

4. Many people think a spider is an _____, but it is not. It has eight legs.

5. People who do not eat meat get _____ from soy, nuts, and beans.

6. Sneezing spreads many _____.

[10] Technology

Getting Ready to Read

A. Learn the words.

Key Vocabulary

common	ordinary; occurring frequently
problem	a difficulty
affordable	not costing much money; cheap; inexpensive

TOEFL Vocabulary

machine	a piece of equipment invented to do a job
workplace	a place where people go to do their jobs
replace	to put a new thing or person in the place of another
impressive	very good; remarkable
operate	to use

B. Learn the question types.

TOEFL Question Types

Inference
Which of the following can be inferred about X?
The author of the passage implies that X . . .

- This type of question asks what is implied, but not stated, in the passage.
- The answer will support or incorporate ideas from the passage.

Rhetorical Purpose
Why does the author mention X?
The author discusses X in order to . . .
The author uses X as an example of . . .

- This question asks why the author has written something in a certain way or why they have used information in a certain place.
- This question also often asks how a statement or paragraph relates to the rest of the passage.

C. Read the passage. Number each paragraph with the correct main idea or purpose.

> 1. The costs of robots
> 2. Future robots
> 3. What robots are
> 4. Robots today

Robots

___Robots are machines that do things people want them to do. They are often used in the workplace.

___Today robots work in factories. They have replaced many people. They make cars and other things. Robots also work in hospitals. They help doctors. These robots are very impressive.

___Robots in the home will be common in the future. They will be easy to operate. These robots may be able to talk. They may clean and lift heavy things. These robots may be able to call for help if there is a problem.

___New robots cost a lot of money. However, robot makers are trying to make them more affordable.

Note-taking

D. Complete the summary notes by filling in the blanks.

Topic: Robots

Introduction: Are _____ that are often used in the _____.

Today: Work in _____.

    • _____ many people

    • Make _____ and other things

Work in _____.

    • Help _____

    • Very _____

In the future: Robots in the home will be _____.

    • Easy to _____

    • Able to _____

    • Clean and lift _____ things

    • Able to call for _____

Robot costs: New robots cost _____.

Trying to make more _____.

E. Choose the correct answers.

1. Which of the following can be inferred about robots?

   (A) A home robot would be good for taking care of small children.

   (B) A home robot would be good for an older person living alone.

2. Why does the author mention robots working in hospitals?

   (A) To show what difficult jobs robots can do.

   (B) To explain how robots have replaced doctors.

3. The author of the passage implies that robots

   (A) are affordable and easy to buy for the home

   (B) are too expensive to buy for the home

4. The author uses talking robots as an example of

   (A) how useful robots may be in the future

   (B) how dangerous robots are

TOEFL Vocabulary Practice

B. Fill in the blanks with the correct words.

machine	workplace	operate	replaced	impressive

1. Robots have _____ many factory workers.

2. A car is a _____ that helps us move around quickly.

3. A hospital is a doctor's _____.

4. Some robots are very difficult to _____.

5. Robots are developing and improving at an _____ speed.

Practice

A. Learn the words.

Key Vocabulary

idea	a thought or concept
zipper	type of fastener that has two rows of teeth that lock together
air conditioning	a system for cooling air

TOEFL Vocabulary

computer	a machine that manages electronic data very quickly
invent	to make a new tool or machine
manufacture	to make a large amount of something to be sold
product	something that is made so it can be sold
provide	to give or supply

B. Read the passage and underline the key information.

Strange Inventions

All inventions start with great ideas. The zipper was a great idea. The computer was too. Many inventions make life better for people. However, some inventions are not very helpful. In fact, they are just strange.

One man did not want spiders to die in his bathtub. He hated the way they got into his tub. They could not get out. Then they died. Therefore, he invented a bathtub spider ladder. Spiders climb the tiny ladder out of the tub. Then they are free.

Another person made something to help smelly feet. He manufactured a product to keep feet dry. It is a little shoe machine. It provides cool air. It is like air conditioning for shoes. This keeps the feet from getting hot and smelly.

The best inventions change the world. However, not all inventions do this. They are just too strange.

C. Choose the correct answers.

1. Which of the following can be inferred about strange inventions?

   (A) Some inventions help very few people.
   (B) They are not useful but are still popular.

2. Why does the author mention the zipper?

   (A) To give an example of a helpful invention.
   (B) To compare a zipper to a computer.

3. Which of the following best expresses the essential information in the highlighted sentence? Incorrect answers change the meaning in important ways or leave out essential information.

   Many inventions make life better for people.

   (A) People like to make inventions.
   (B) Many people's lives have been improved by inventions.
   (C) To have a better life, you must make an invention.
   (D) Inventions are not popular for many people.

TOEFL Vocabulary Practice

D. Fill in the blanks with the correct words.

computers	invented	manufacture	product	provide

1. Oil is a _____ that is sold in barrels.

2. Many computer companies _____ technical support with their products.

3. Jack Kilby _____ the microchip in 1959.

4. NASA could not have gone to the moon without _____.

5. Some automakers are racing to _____ cars that will only cost three thousand dollars each.

Test

Read the passage.

How Radio Was Developed

Radio is an impressive invention. It took many ideas to invent the radio.

Before radio, messages were sent over wires. This was how the telephone worked. However, using wires to send messages was not always possible. So, people wanted to replace this system. By the late 1800s, inventors learned something. They learned that sound could be sent in waves. These waves went through the air. Then people could receive them far away. Still, this was not easy to do. Some stopped trying. Others didn't stop.

■ 1) Tesla was an inventor. ■ 2) He did not give up. He kept trying. He found a way to send radio waves. They went through the air. ■ 3) They went very far. They also went very fast. This had never been done. ■ 4)

Marconi was an inventor too. He also kept trying. He was good at science. He was the first person to send a message across the Atlantic Ocean. He made a business in 1907. This provided radio stations for ships to use. It made ship travel safer. It also saved many lives.

Later, many signals could be sent at the same time. This is how radio stations were started. People could buy machines to listen to these signals. Hundreds of these machines were manufactured.

People use the radio for news. They use it for music too. The radio is very common today. This is because it is affordable. It is also very easy to operate.

Choose the correct answers.

1. Which of the following best expresses the essential information in the highlighted sentence? Incorrect answers change the meaning in important ways or leave out essential information.

   So, people wanted to replace this system.

   (A) People wanted to find a way to send better messages.
   (B) People wanted to buy new radios for sending messages.
   (C) People wanted to find a way to send messages without wires.
   (D) People wanted to find something that would replace electricity.

2. According to the passage, the radio is very common today because

    (A) it is cheap and easy to use

    (B) many people travel by ship

    (C) there are many radio stations

    (D) many signals can be sent at the same time

3. Look at the four squares that indicate where the following sentence could be added to the passage.

This is why many people feel Tesla is radio's true inventor.

Where would the sentence best fit?

    (A) Square 1   (B) Square 2

    (C) Square 3   (D) Square 4

4. Why does the author mention radio stations for ships?

    (A) To explain how many ships used radio stations

    (B) To give an example of how radio made things safer

    (C) To show how Marconi started a shipping business

    (D) To discuss one of the many ways radios were being used

5. The word signals is closest in meaning to

    (A) letters   (R) radio waves

    (C) songs   (D) radio

6. Directions: Complete the table below about the inventors discussed in the passage. Match the statements to the correct inventor. TWO of the answer choices will NOT be used.

Answer choices

    (A) Made a radio business for ships

    (B) Was very good at science

    (C) Sent a radio message across the Atlantic

    (D) Before him, radio waves had never been sent through the air.

    (E) Discovered electricity

    (F) Found a way to send radio waves

    (G) Used impressive machines

Tesla
- _____
- _____

Marconi
- _____
- _____
- _____

Check-up

A. Choose the correct answers.

1. An inference question asks

   (A) what can be implied from the passage
   (B) what a word or phrase means
   (C) why the author has written something in a certain way or in a certain place
   (D) about details or facts that are in the passage

2. A rhetorical purpose question asks

   (A) for another sentence to be placed into the passage
   (B) what can be implied from the passage
   (C) what a word or phrase refers to in the passage
   (D) why the author has written something in a certain way or in a certain place

Key Vocabulary Practice

B. Fill in the blanks with the correct words.

common	problems	idea	affordable	zippers	air conditioning

1. _____ has made life more comfortable for many people in hot countries.

2. The shape of a light bulb is often used to symbolize an _____.

3. Before _____ were invented, most people used buttons to fasten their clothes.

4. The newest technology often takes years before it is _____ enough to buy.

5. Today safety pins are quite _____, but this invention didn't exist before 1849.

6. Inventors often have many _____ when they invent something new.

[11] Geography

Getting Ready to Read

A. Learn the words.

Key Vocabulary

wine	alcoholic drink made from grapes
famous	known to many
festival	a party or feast that celebrates something

TOEFL Vocabulary

border	the boundary of a country
moderate	temperate; not extreme
tropical	relating to the area near the equator, hot and humid
climate	how hot or cold, dry or rainy a place is; the weather
travel	to journey or visit another place

B. Learn the question type.

TOEFL Question Type

Insert Text

Look at the four squares that indicate where the following sentence could be added to the passage.

[You will see a sentence in bold.]

Where would the sentence best fit?

- This type of question asks for another sentence to be placed into the passage.
- The answer will connect logically and grammatically to the sentences on either side.

C. Read the passage. Number each paragraph with the correct main idea or purpose.

> 1. Moldova's weather
> 2. Money in Moldova
> 3. Where Moldova is
> 4. Farming in Moldova

Moldova

___ ■ **1)** Moldova is a small country. ■ **2)** It is in Eastern Europe. ■ **3)** It shares a border with two other countries. ■ **4)**

___ Moldova has moderate weather. ■ **5)** The summers are warm. They are not hot. ■ **6)** People who don't like tropical climates will like it. ■ **7)** The winters there are not very cold. ■ **8)**

___ Moldova has good farmland. Farmers grow fruit. The fruit is made into wine. Moldova is very famous for wine. Anyone who travels there should go in October. That is when the wine festival is.

___ Moldova is also a cheap country to travel in. It is not expensive to buy things there.

D. Complete the summary notes by filling in the blanks.

Topic:	Moldova
Where:	Small country in Eastern _____.
	Border with _____ countries.
Weather:	Is _____.
	• Warm _____, not hot
	• Winters not very _____
Farming:	Good _____.
	Farmers grow fruit, which is made into _____.
	_____ for wine.
	Wine festival is in _____.
Money:	_____ to travel in.
	Not expensive to _____ things.

E. **Choose the correct answers.**

1. Look at the four squares (■) that indicate where the following sentence could be added to the passage.

    Its neighbors are Romania and the Ukraine.

    Where would the sentence best fit?

    (A) Square 1   (B) Square 2
    (C) Square 3   (D) Square 4

2. Look at the four squares (■) that indicate where the following sentence could be added to the passage.

    So, people who do not like a lot of snow would like it there.

    Where would the sentence best fit?

    (A) Square 5   (B) Square 6
    (C) Square 7   (D) Square 8

TOEFL Vocabulary Practice

F. **Fill in the blanks with the correct words.**

moderate	border	tropical	traveled	climate

1. Panmunjom is a town on the _____ of North and South Korea.

2. Hawaii has a _____ climate.

3. The problem with _____ winters is that there is no snow for skiing.

4. A moderate _____ is good for growing wheat.

5. Marco Polo _____ from Italy to China.

Practice

A. Learn the words.

Key Vocabulary

system	parts placed together to form a working unit
satellite	something that orbits the Earth
receiver	machine that takes in information

TOEFL Vocabulary

global	worldwide
information	knowledge; facts and data
prevent	to stop something from happening
practical	workable; good and easy to use
geography	the study of the Earth including how it is divided, its climates, and resources

B. Read the passage and underline the key information.

GPS

GPS is a system. It means "Global Positioning System." It helps people find out where they are. Let's see how it works.

■ **1)** There are machines called satellites in the sky. ■ **2)** They move around Earth. ■ **3)** They send information to small machines on Earth. These machines are called GPS receivers. ■ **4)**

GPS receivers can tell you many things. They can tell you where you are. They can tell you how fast you are going. They also tell you where you are going. They prevent you from getting lost.

They are very practical. These days they are common. They are good tools for people who study geography. GPS can help to make maps. GPS is used in cars and airplanes. You can use the GPS receiver in your car. It can find a place you are driving to. Hikers use GPS receivers. Then they don't get lost in the mountains.

C. Choose the correct answers.

1. Look at the four squares (■) that indicate where the following sentence could be added to the passage.

They are like big flying computers.

Where would the sentence best fit?

(A) Square 1   (B) Square 2
(C) Square 3   (D) Square 4

2. Which of the following can be inferred about most GPS receivers?

(A) They are very expensive.
(B) They are usually small.
(C) They are usually very big.
(D) They are not very useful to most people.

3. The author discusses using GPS in your car in order to

(A) explain how cars work
(B) explain why so many people get lost while driving cars
(C) explain why GPS is expensive
(D) show how GPS can be useful in everyday activities

TOEFL Vocabulary Practice

D. Fill in the blanks with the correct words.

geography	practical	prevent	global	information

1. Computers can share _____ at a very high speed.

2. The British Prime Minister did not _____ Hitler from invading Czechoslovakia.

3. The Internet is a _____ computer network.

4. In _____ class, we learn about the weather and maps.

5. A Swiss army knife is a very _____ tool.

Read the passage.

City Life and Country Life

City life and country life are very different. People who study geography look at these differences. They study why people move to cities. The reasons are practical. People go to cities to look for work.

Moving to the city is very easy. It isn't like moving to another country. You don't have to cross a border. You just go.

A city is like a system. Roads and subways are part of the system. So are apartments and shopping malls. They form a unit. This unit makes life easy for city people. They can travel to work quickly on the subway. They can also drive around. They can buy many things in supermarkets. There are good schools in the city.

Country life is simple. However, it is hard work. It is the same in most climates. It is not crowded. There is a lot of space, so everything is far apart. People walk to work. They sometimes ride horses. Often there are only a few trains and cars.

Farmers grow fruit and vegetables to eat. ■ 1) They keep animals. ■ 2) There are not many supermarkets. ■ 3) People often know everyone who lives nearby. ■ 4) At harvest time, there is often a harvest festival. People store food for winter time. It is hard to grow vegetables when the weather is cold.

Many people in the country are poor. They want to leave and move to the cities. City people want to prevent this. There will be no one to grow food. The cities will also become too crowded.

Choose the correct answers.

1. Why does the author mention borders?

(A) Because you need to cross a border to move to the city.

(B) Because sometimes people move to cities in a different country.

(C) Because he wants to show that moving to the city is easy.

(D) Because he thinks cities should have borders.

2. The word unit in the passage is closest in meaning to

(A) a whole   (B) a number

(C) a country   (D) a machine

3. Which of the following best expresses the essential information in the highlighted sentence? Incorrect answers change the meaning in important ways or leave out essential information.

They can buy many things in supermarkets.

(A) People steal food from shops.
(B) Many things in supermarkets are expensive.
(C) Supermarkets sell many different products.
(D) Farmers go to the city to buy things.

4. According to the passage, all the following are mentioned as part of the city system EXCEPT

(A) roads   (B) churches
(C) shopping malls   (D) apartments

5. Look at the four squares (■) that indicate where the following sentence could be added to the passage.

Fresh farm food is very healthy.

Where would the sentence best fit?

(A) Square 1   (B) Square 2
(C) Square 3   (D) Square 4

6. Directions: An introductory sentence for a brief summary of the passage is provided below. Complete the summary by selecting the THREE answer choices that express the most important ideas in the passage. Some sentences do not belong in the summary because they express ideas that are not presented in the passage or are minor ideas in the passage.

There are many differences between living in the country and in the city.

Answer choices

(A) Life in the countryside is slower and harder but healthier than city life.
(B) You do not need a passport to live in the city.
(C) There are few trains and supermarkets in the country.
(D) People want to live in cities to find work but not everyone can live there.
(E) Cities are like systems with many parts that help people who live there.

Check-up

A. Choose the correct answers.

1. An *insert text* question asks

    (A) for another sentence to be placed into the passage

    (B) for the main ideas in the passage to be identified

    (C) for a sentence to be removed from the passage

    (D) for major ideas and important information to be categorized

Key Vocabulary Practice

B. Fill in the blanks with the correct words.

satellite	famous	festival	receivers	system	wine

1. Pilots use radio _____ to talk to people on the ground.

2. The moon is a natural _____.

3. Our solar _____ has nine planets.

4. The Korean harvest _____ is called Chuseok.

5. _____ is made from grapes.

6. David Beckham is a _____ soccer player.

[12] Music

Getting Ready to Read

A. Learn the words.

Key Vocabulary

string	a long cord stretched across a musical instrument
bow	a short pole with horsehair stretched between the ends that is used to play many instruments
hammer	a tool for hitting something

TOEFL Vocabulary

instrument	a thing used to make sounds and music
variety	a wide range of differences; a certain type
quality	a physical, mental, or emotional trait
arrange	to place in a certain order
possess	to have

B. Learn the question type.

TOEFL Question Type

Table

Directions: Complete the table below   to summarize information about X
                                           by matching X with Y
                                           by selecting X

TWO of the answer choices will NOT be used.

- This type of question asks for major ideas and important information to be categorized.
- The incorrect answer choices will state information that is not mentioned or is not relevant to the categories.

C. Read the passage. Number each paragraph with the correct main idea or purpose.

1. Information about plucked instruments
2. Information about struck instruments
3. Information about bowed instruments
4. Information about stringed instruments

Stringed Instruments

___Stringed instruments use moving strings. They have a variety of sound qualities. There are three kinds of stringed instruments. They are arranged by how they are played.

___Some instruments are plucked. Plucking is pulling something with the fingers. Guitar strings are plucked.

___Some instruments are played by bowing them. The strings are moved with a bow. The bow is pulled across the strings. The violin and the cello is bowed.

___The last kind of stringed instrument is played by hitting the strings. This is called striking. For example, the piano possesses small hammers. They strike the strings to make them move.

Note-taking

D. Complete the summary notes by filling in the blanks.

Topic:	Stringed Instruments
Introduction:	Use moving strings.
	Have a _____ of sound qualities.
	_____ kinds.
	• _____ by how they are played
Plucked:	Plucking is _____ something with the fingers.
	_____ are plucked.
Bowed:	Strings are moved with a _____.
	The bow is _____ across the strings.
	The violin and cello are bowed.
Struck:	Played by _____ the strings.
	The piano _____ small hammers.
	• Hit the strings to make them _____

E. Choose the correct answers.

1. Directions: Complete the table below about the stringed instruments discussed in the passage. Match the statements to the correct stringed instrument. TWO of the answer choices will NOT be used.

Answer choices

(A) Uses a special pole to move strings

(B) Moves strings by stretching them

(C) Moves strings by hitting them

(D) Uses fingers to move strings

(E) Moves something across strings

(F) Needs a combination of bowing and plucking

(G) Uses hammers to move strings

Plucked
• _____

Bowed
• _____
• _____

Struck
• _____
• _____

TOEFL Vocabulary Practice

F. Fill in the blanks with the correct words.

arranged	instrument	possesses	quality	variety

1. The flute is widely believed to be the world's oldest kind of _____.

2. The double bass has the deepest sound _____ of any stringed instrument.

3. A choir is typically _____ into four main sections.

4. A woodwind instrument sometimes _____ up to six different reeds.

5. The harmonica, a _____ of wind instrument, was first made in 1857.

Practice

A. Learn the words.

Key Vocabulary

band	musicians playing together
tone	a particular kind of sound
record	a vinyl disc that is played to listen to a song; any song

TOEFL Vocabulary

talent	a natural ability to do something
entertain	to do something such as act or sing for others' enjoyment
reputation	the opinion others have about something or someone
unique	one of a kind; special
control	precision

B. Read the passage and underline the key information.

Ella Fitzgerald

Ella Fitzgerald was a talented jazz singer. As a child, she was very poor. However, by the time she was 21, her style had made her famous.

Ella loved to entertain people, and they loved her happy sound. Ella's voice made even sad songs sound happy. This cheerful sound made her popular. This style gave Ella the reputation of being unique.

Another part of Ella's style was the way she would "scat." Scatting is making up words or sounds that don't make sense. She used her voice as an instrument this way. She said she tried to do what the instruments in the band were doing.

Ella never had any voice training. ■ 1) However, her singing was excellent. ■ 2) She had very good tone and control. ■ 3) Also, people loved how clearly she sang. ■ 4) She sold forty million records because of her style.

C. **Choose the correct answers.**

1. Look at the four squares (■) that indicate where the following sentence could be added to the passage.

   Ella was very successful.

   Where would the sentence best fit?

   (A) Square 1   (B) Square 2
   (C) Square 3   (D) Square 4

2. **Directions:** Complete the table below about Ella Fitzgerald's style discussed in the passage. Match the characteristic to the correct style. TWO of the answer choices will NOT be used.

   Answer choices

   (A) Made up words
   (B) Tried to sound like other singers
   (C) Had professional training
   (D) Used her voice as an instrument
   (E) Had a cheerful style
   (F) Sang clearly
   (G) Made sad songs seem happy
   (H) Tried to sound like musical instruments
   (I) Had excellent tone and control

   Sound
   * _____
   * _____

   Scat Style
   * _____
   * _____
   * _____

   Skills
   * _____
   * _____

D. **Fill in the blanks with the correct words.**

reputation	entertained	talent	unique	control

1. Many people thought that Ella Fitzgerald's cheerful singing was _____.

2. It takes natural _____ and training to become an opera singer.

3. Oprah Winfrey has a good _____ because she helps many people.

4. The Beatles were a famous British band who often _____ huge audiences.

5. Celine Dion is a singer with great voice _____.

Read the passage.

DJs

Disc jockeys are called DJs for short. What is a DJ? A DJ plays records. DJs were not very important at first. Many people thought they possessed no talent. This is because they just arranged the order of songs on the radio. However, DJs soon became very important. They changed music in three ways.

First, DJs made the radio popular again. People used to listen to the radio a lot. They liked the news. They also liked funny shows. Then, in the early 1950s people started watching more television. People did not listen to the radio as much. Radio stations had to find a new way to entertain people. People still liked music. Therefore, radio DJs played more songs. They also talked in between the songs. People liked this.

Next, DJs made new music popular. ■ 1) For example, DJs chose which songs to play more. ■ 2) They also changed the variety of music. ■ 3) DJs helped make rock 'n' roll popular. ■ 4) People still love rock 'n' roll. It changed music today.

Last, DJs invented rap music. They did this by playing songs in a new way. They scratched records on a record player. Scratching is playing a small piece of a song over and over. This gives the music a different sound quality. This was a new sound. It helped make the style of rap. It is still a big part of rap music today.

DJs did a lot with music. They changed it forever. Music is always changing. DJs help it change.

Choose the correct answers.

1. According to paragraph 2, what can be inferred about radio?

   (A) It was invented before television was invented.
   (B) It was more popular than the television in the 1950s.
   (C) It is more important than television is today.
   (D) Its invention was the result of disc jockeys.

2. The word they in the passage refers to

   (A) people
   (B) songs
   (C) DJs
   (D) stations

3. According to the passage, all of the following are true about DJs EXCEPT

(A) they changed the reasons that people listened to radios

(B) they influenced why radios played funny shows

(C) they impacted which kind of music was popular

(D) they helped radio be more popular

4. Look at the four squares (■) that indicate where the following sentence could be added to the passage.

Typically, these were the most popular songs.

Where would the sentence best fit?

(A) Square 1   (B) Square 2

(C) Square 3   (D) Square 4

5. Which of the following best expresses the essential information in the highlighted sentence? Incorrect answers change the meaning in important ways or leave out essential information.

It changed music today.

(A) Music was greatly affected by rock 'n' roll.

(B) The rock 'n' roll recordings are not as good without DJs.

(C) Rock 'n' roll techniques are included in all kinds of music now.

(D) DJs made rock 'n' roll more popular than any kind of music since.

6. Directions: An introductory sentence for a brief summary of the passage is provided below. Complete the summary by selecting the THREE answer choices that express the most important ideas in the passage. Some sentences do not belong in the summary because they express ideas that are not presented in the passage or are minor ideas in the passage.

DJs affected the history of music in several ways.

Answer choices

(A) They played tracks over and over.

(B) They influenced what kind of music became successful.

(C) They developed rap music.

(D) They played songs in different ways.

(E) They made the radio popular with people again.

Check-up

A. Choose the correct answer.

1. A *table* questions asks
   - (A) for specific details or facts that are in the passage
   - (B) for another sentence to be placed into the passage
   - (C) for the main ideas in the passage to be identified
   - (D) for major ideas and important information to be categorized

Key Vocabulary Practice

B. Fill in the blanks with the correct words.

bow	record	strings	hammer	band	tone

1. A piano has many _____ for the hammers to strike.

2. The Beatles is a famous _____ from Liverpool, England.

3. A bell usually has a very clear _____.

4. A new violin and _____ are very expensive.

5. A dulcimer is played by hitting the strings with a _____.

6. Elton John's song *Candle in the Wind* is the most bought _____ of all time.

[Review 2]

Read the passage.

Pittsburgh

Today Pittsburgh does not have a reputation as a great international city. However, 100 years ago, it did. It was one of the most important cities in America.

Pittsburgh has advantageous geography. This is because it was built on three rivers. This allowed it to efficiently ship its products along its rivers. It also has a lot of coal. This could be used for fuel.

This let Pittsburgh become a center for manufacturing. Its most famous product was steel. Its nickname is "The Steel City." This city was also a center for banking, chemical, and food manufacturing.

Many rich and famous people lived there. They set up many important companies. Andrew Carnegie made millions of dollars from steel. Henry J. Heinz created the Heinz Company. It is famous for ketchup. Charles Schwab made a bank in Pittsburgh. George Westinghouse started an electric company. It invented air brakes for cars and trains. It also helped to put power into every home.

After 1950, Pittsburgh started to struggle. ■ 1) Other cities were discovering ways to efficiently manufacture steel. ■ 2) Pittsburgh also struggled with pollution. This made many people move away. ■ 3)

It may not be as well known today but Pittsburgh has an impressive history. ■ 4)

Choose the correct answers.

1. The word ship in the passage is closest in meaning to
   (A) a big boat
   (B) moving products from one city to another
   (C) making products
   (D) buying products

2. According to the passage, Heinz Company is famous for
   (A) steel   (B) banking
   (C) air Brakes   (D) ketchup

3. Which of these things did Pittsburgh NOT have one hundred years ago?

(A) Rich citizens   (B) Three rivers

(C) Large Companies   (D) Pollution

4. Which of the following best expresses the essential information in the highlighted sentence? Incorrect answers change the meaning in important ways or leave out essential information.

Other cities were discovering ways to efficiently manufacture steel.

(A) Other cities could not make steel.

(B) Other cities learned to make steel quickly.

(C) Other cities learned to buy cheap steel quickly.

(D) Other cities slowly learned how to make steel.

5. The author of the passage implies that Pittsburgh

(A) will never become a great city again

(B) is still polluted and ugly

(C) has made many important contributions to America

(D) is still one of the most important cities in America

6. Look at the four squares (■) that indicate where the following sentence could be added to the passage.

This made many factories struggle, so many people lost their jobs.

Where would the sentence best fit?

(A) Square 1   (B) Square 2

(C) Square 3   (D) Square 4

Read the passage.

MP3 players

Now it seems everyone has an MP3 player. MP3 players are popular with all ages of people. They are small. They let you organize and arrange thousands of songs. You can also keep a large variety of music on it. They also work with computers. This makes it very easy to get songs. You can also share songs with friends. This lets you make unique play lists.

■ **1)** MP3 players are only the newest portable music players. ■ **2)** There is a long history of music players. The first popular portable machine was the radio. They were small. This made it easy to carry. ■ **3)** However, they didn't work in the country. You had to be in or near a city to hear music on the radio. ■ **4)**

After radios came cassette players. They were great. They let people choose their own music. They also let people listen to the radio. People often used them while they exercised. They had problems, though. Cassettes sometimes broke. They also lost their music quality. This happened after they were played a lot. It also took a while to find the song you wanted.

CD players replaced cassette players. Many preferred CD players. They had a reputation for possessing high quality sound. They also efficiently found songs. However, they had a problem. A person could only play a few songs on one CD. This caused others to invent MP3 players.

Choose the correct answers.

1. Why does the author use the word only in the following sentence?

   MP3 players are only the newest portable music players.

   (A) The author wants to show that lots of people have MP3 players.
   (B) The author wants to show that there have been many other portable players.
   (C) The author wants to explain that there is one kind of MP3 player.
   (D) The author wants to introduce MP3 players to everyone.

2. The word portable is closest in meaning to
   (A) loudest   (B) high tech
   (C) easily moved   (D) advantageous

3. Look at the four squares (■) that indicate where the following sentence could be added to the passage.

With all the great things MP3 players can do, it is hard to imagine music before them.

Where would the sentence fit best?

(A) Square 1   (B) Square 2

(C) Square 3   (D) Square 4

4. Which of the following does they refer to?

(A) cassettes   (B) cassette players

(C) music quality   (D) radios

5. The most popular portable music players before MP3 players were

(A) cassette players   (B) radios

(C) CD players   (D) computers

6. Which of the following best expresses the essential information in the highlighted sentence? Incorrect answers change the meaning in important ways or leave out essential information.

They had a reputation for possessing high quality sound.

(A) CD's were known for being fast.

(B) People thought CD's were really cool.

(C) CD's were known for having great sound.

(D) CD's were fast, but the sound was not that good.

Read the passage.

Diabetes

Diabetes is a disease that affects 7% of all Americans. People with diabetes are called diabetics. The number of diabetics increases each year.

Diabetes has two forms. They are called "type one" and "type two." Diabetes prevents the body from using the chemical called insulin. Insulin changes sugar into fuel. However, diabetics cannot use sugar efficiently.

The cause of diabetes is unknown. Overweight people are at greater risk. Also, parents tend to pass it down to their children. Exercise and eating healthy food are important. These are great ways to help prevent diabetes.

Diabetes can be very dangerous. People with it must be treated. People with diabetes can go into "shock." This is when there isn't enough sugar in a person's blood. Shock can be prevented. This is done by always having orange juice or crackers to eat.

Fortunately, it is easily treated. Scientists discovered how to manufacture insulin. Diabetics give themselves shots everyday. These are usually in the leg, bottom, or stomach. They also have to test their blood. They do this often during the day. This controls the amount of sugar in the blood.

Diabetics can also keep good health by eating well. Doctors encourage them to decrease the amount of sweet foods. Sweet foods make it hard to control.

Diabetics can have normal lives. They have to be careful and responsible. However, many have become famous actors, singers, and scientists.

Choose the correct answers.

1. What does the phrase tend to pass it down mean?

(A) Children can sometimes have similar diseases as their parents.
(B) Parents can make children have diabetes.
(C) Parents can prevent children from having diabetes.
(D) Children take diabetes from their parents.

2. The word these in the sentence refers to

(A) insulin   (B) diabetes
(C) food   (D) shots

3. Diabetes can be controlled by all the ways EXCEPT

    (A) getting insulin shots

    (B) not eating sugary foods

    (C) testing their blood

    (D) going into "shock"

4. What can be implied from the following sentence?

However, many have become famous actors, singers, and scientists.

    (A) People can still have very successful lives even with diabetes.

    (B) Singers, actors, and scientists have to work harder because they have diabetes.

    (C) Diabetes helps to make people successful.

    (D) Diabetes stops many people from being actors.

5. Why does the author include the first paragraph in this passage?

    (A) The author wants to tell people about diabetes.

    (B) The author wants to show how big of a disease diabetes is.

    (C) The author wants the number of diabetics to decrease.

    (D) The author wants to help people with diabetes.

6. **Directions:** Complete the table below about the aspects of diabetes discussed in the passage. Match the statements to the correct aspect of diabetes. TWO of the answer choices will NOT be used.

Answer choices

    (A) Exercising

    (B) Eating less sugary food

    (C) Being overweight

    (D) Taking shots of insulin

    (E) Eating some sugar

    (F) Become an actor

    (G) Parents having diabetes

Causes of diabetes

- _____
- _____

Controlling diabetes

- _____
- _____
- _____

Basic Skills for the
TOEFL® iBT 1

Moraig Macgillivray
Kayang Gagiano

Reading

Transcript & Answer Key

Answer Key

[Unit 1]

Getting Ready

Page 14

C

3, 4, 2, 1

D

Topic:	Joseph Stalin
Introduction:	<u>Well-known</u> leader of the Soviet Union from 1928 to <u>1953</u>.
Name:	Called <u>Iosif</u> Dzhugashvili. Changed his name to <u>Stalin</u>. Means "man of <u>steel</u>" in Russian. Wanted people to think he was a <u>strong</u> leader.
Impact:	<u>Changed</u> the country. • From a <u>nation</u> based on <u>agriculture</u> • To a nation based on <u>industry</u> Forced farm w<u>orkers</u> to work in <u>factories</u>.
Conclusion:	Was <u>cruel</u>. Killed many to get what he wanted.

Page 15

E

1. A   2. A   3. B   4. A

F

1. nation   2. industry   3. leader
4. impact   5. agriculture

Practice

Page 17

C

1. B   2. A   3. B   4. B

D

1. resource   2. archaeologist   3. conclusion
4. consists   5. traded

Test

Page 18

1. C   2. C   3. D   4. C
5. A   6. C, E, A

Check-up

Page 20

A

1. A   2. D

B

1. factory   2. well-known   3. mine
4. cruel   5. pottery   6. ruins

[Unit 2]

Getting Ready

Page 22

C

4, 3, 2, 1

D

Topic:	Modern Art
Introduction:	Art comes from the <u>imagination</u>. In the 19th <u>century</u> painters <u>imagined</u> new ways to <u>paint</u>.
Beginnings:	Painters were <u>tired</u> of painting the same way. Most thought paintings should look <u>real</u>. Painters made people and things look <u>odd</u>.
Painting styles:	Some used odd <u>colors</u>. Others threw <u>paint</u> on canvases. Others painted things like <u>soup cans</u>.
Critics:	At first, people <u>did not</u> like this kind of art. Then, people began to <u>understand</u> and like modern art.

Page 23

E

1. A   2. B   3. B   4. A

F

1. formal   2. century   3. imagine
4. inspire   5. odd

Answer Key

Practice

Page 25

C

1. A 2. B 3. B 4. B

D

1. pose 2. blend 3. normal
4. introduce 5. style

Test

Page 26

1. A 2. D 3. C 4. D
5. B 6. A, D, E

Check-up

Page 28

A

1. A 2. C

B

1. canvas 2. dot 3. Modern art
4. strokes 5. pure 6. tired

[Unit 3]

Getting Ready

Page 30

C

2, 3, 4, 1

D

Topic: Polar Bears
Introduction: Have white <u>fur</u>.
Live near the <u>North Pole</u> in <u>extreme</u> <u>weather</u>.
Hunting: Not much <u>food</u>.
Like to <u>hunt</u> seals but hard to find.
Often eat other <u>animals</u>.
Have to hunt <u>carefully</u>.
White fur: White fur helps to <u>blend in</u> with surroundings.
White fur is same color as <u>snow</u>.

Hunting: When it has an opportunity, the bear will <u>attack</u> a seal.
- Cannot see bears in <u>time</u>
- <u>Surprise</u> for them
White fur helps polar bears <u>hunt</u>.

Page 31

E

1. A 2. B

F

1. surroundings 2. attacked 3. extreme
4. opportunity 5. determine

Practice

Page 33

C

1. B 2. A 3. B

D

1. rare 2. gather 3. prepare
4. protect 5. shelters

Test

Page 34

1. D 2. C 3. D
4. B 5. A

6. **Skunks**
- (B) Small animal
- (D) Uses spray for protection .
- (F) Protects its shelter

Buffalo
- (A) Large animal
- (C) Gather in herds

Check-up

Page 36

A

1. D

B

1. wake up 2. hibernate 3. blending in
4. caves 5. hunting 6. fur

[Unit 4]

Getting Ready

Page 38

C

4, 3, 1, 2

D

Topic:	Physics
Introduction:	<u>Physics</u> is a science.
	Looks at <u>energy</u> and matter.
	Studies light, heat, sound, <u>electricity</u> and, mechanics.
Energy:	<u>Energy</u> is the way things move and how work is done.
	<u>Some</u> things have a lot of energy. Some do not
Matter:	Matter is what things are <u>made</u> of. Solids, liquids, and gasses are all <u>matter</u>.
Heat:	Heat is <u>energy</u>. This energy makes water <u>boil</u>. Scientists <u>measure</u> energy and matter.

Page 39

E

1. A   2. B   3. A   4. A

F

1. measure   2. electricity   3. mechanics
4. physics   5. energy

Practice

Page 41

C

1. A   2. B   3. B

D

1. transfer   2. destroyed   3. result
4. potential   5. object

Test

Page 42

1. A   2. B   3. B   4. A
5. D   6. A, C, D

Check-up

Page 44

A

1. C   2. A

B

1. gas   2. passing   3. solid
4. kinetic   5. liquid   6. moving

[Unit 5]

Getting Ready

Page 46

C

3, 4, 1, 2

D

Topic:	Starting a Business
Introduction:	Can be hard work.
	A lot of <u>details</u>.
	A lot to do before <u>selling</u> things.
What to sell:	Decide what to <u>sell</u>.
	Decide what to <u>charge</u>
Name:	<u>Choose</u> a name.
	- Is important
	- Lets people <u>know</u> about your business
Website:	Let's people find out about your <u>business</u>.

Page 47

E

1. B   2. D

F

1. charge   2. choose   3. decide
4. business   5. detail

Practice

Page 49

C

1. D   2. A   3. A

D

1. company   2. example   3. goal
4. advertise   5. original

Answer Key

Test

Page 50

1. C   2. B   3. D   4. C
5. B   6. A, B, C

Check-up

Page 52

A

1. D

B

1. website   2. sign   3. sells
4. hard work   5. buy   6. curious

[Unit 6]

Getting Ready

Page 54

C

2, 4, 1, 3, 5

D

Topic:	The sun
Introduction:	Is a <u>star</u>.
	Is a <u>giant</u> circle of burning <u>gas</u>.
	Has three main <u>parts</u>.
First Segment:	Solar <u>core</u>
	- Deep <u>inside</u>
	- Extremely <u>hot</u>
Second Segment:	<u>Surface</u>
	- Called photosphere
	- <u>Cooler</u> than core
Third Segment:	Atmosphere
	- Called <u>corona</u>
	- Can't see it from <u>Earth</u>
Conclusion:	Will change and <u>eventually</u> die.
	Does not have enough <u>energy</u> to <u>survive</u>.

Page 55

E

1. A, B, E   2. A, C, D

F

1. survived   2. surface   3. core
4. segments   5. Eventually

Practice

Page 57

C

1. D   2. B, C, E

D

1. events   2. outline   3. Astronomy
4. entire   5. blocked

Test

Page 58

1. D   2. A   3. D   4. C
5. B   6. A, D, E

Check-up

Page 60

A

1. C

B

1. atmosphere   2. solar   3. orbit
4. partial   5. inside   6. total

[Review 1]

Reading 1

Page 61

1. B   2. A   3. A   4. D   5. B   6. C

Reading 2

Page 63

1. D   2. C   3. B   4. C   5. A, C, D

Reading 3

Page 65

1. C   2. C   3. D   4. D   5. B   6. B

[Unit 7]

Getting Ready

Page 68

C

2, 3, 1, 4

D

Topic:	Bestsellers
Introduction:	Many books are <u>printed</u> but only a few become <u>popular</u>. Bestsellers are <u>books</u> that sell a lot of <u>copies</u>.
Bestseller Lists:	<u>Organized</u> by how many sold. Sell the most = first on list.
Bestseller:	Harry Potter is one of most <u>famous</u> bestsellers. - A boy's <u>struggle</u> against bad people - <u>Character</u> very well known
Copies:	Sell more than most books. Harry Potter sold <u>107</u> million. - One of the most <u>popular</u> ever

Page 69

E

1. B   2. B   3. A   4. A

F

1. organized   2. characters   3. struggles
4. popular   5. described

Practice

Page 71

C

1. B   2. A   3. A, C, D

D

1. literature   2. crimes   3. treated
4. published   5. issue

Test

Page 72

1. C   2. C   3. D   4. A
5. A   6. A, D, E

Check-up

Page 74

A

1. D   2. B

B

1. suspect   2. trial   3. copy
4. successful   5. print   6. list

[Unit 8]

Getting Ready

Page 76

C

3, 2, 1, 5, 4

D

Topic:	Whaling
Introduction:	Humpback whales - <u>one</u> of oceans most beautiful <u>animals</u>. Most were <u>killed</u>.
Whale hunting:	Whales hunted for <u>food</u>, tools, and <u>clothes</u>.
Effects of Harpoon:	In late <u>1880s</u> new <u>harpoon</u> was made. - Killed whales more <u>efficiently</u> People hunted a lot more whales. By 1966, <u>90%</u> of <u>planet's</u> humpback whales dead.
Whaling laws:	<u>International</u> law banned the hunting of whales. Some people still try to <u>hunt</u> whales

Page 77

E

1. B   2. B   3. A   4. A

F

1. banned   2. planet   3. law
4. international 5. efficiently

Practice

Page 79

C

1. B   2. B   3. A   4. A

Answer Key

D

1. pollution   2. decrease   3. fuel
4. discovered   5. advantageous

Test

Page 80

1. C   2. A   3. D   4. A
5. C   6. B, C, D

Check-up

Page 82

A

1. C   2. A

B

1. smoke   2. tools   3. gasoline
4. oceans   5. harpoon   6. garbage

[Unit 9]

Getting Ready

Page 84

C

4, 3, 1, 2

D

Topic:	Exercise
Introduction:	Is great for the <u>body</u> and <u>mind</u>.
	Some do not like to exercise.
	Those who exercise feel <u>good</u>.
Body:	Makes <u>muscles</u> strong, keeps body lean, makes heart <u>healthy</u>.
	Strong heart is an important <u>effect</u> of exercise.
Mind:	Helps the <u>brain</u> make <u>chemicals</u>.
	- Makes people feel <u>happy</u>.
	Sad or angry people feel <u>better</u> when they exercise.
How often:	Doctors <u>encourage</u> people to exercise <u>three</u> times a week.
	- Can be <u>hard</u>
	- <u>Rewards</u> are great
	The body and <u>mind</u> need exercise.

Page 85

E

1. B   2. A

F

1. chemical   2. effect   3. encourage
4. health   5. reward

Practice

Page 87

C

1. A   2. B   3. B

D

1. refuse   2. prefer   3. Vitamin
4. society   5. For instance

Test

Page 88

1. A   2. D   3. A   4. C
5. C   6. A, C, D

Check-up

Page 90

A

1. C

B

1. brain   2. mind   3. lean
4. insect   5. protein   6. germs

[Unit 10]

Getting Ready

Page 92

C

3, 4, 2, 1

D

Topic:	Robots
Introduction:	Are <u>machines</u> that are often used in the <u>workplace</u>.
Today:	Work in <u>factories</u>.
	- <u>Replaced</u> many people
	- Make <u>cars</u> and other things
	Work in <u>hospitals</u>.
	- Help <u>doctors</u>
	- Very <u>impressive</u>

In the future:	Robots in the home will be <u>common</u>.
	- Easy to <u>operate</u>
	- Able to <u>talk</u>
	- Clean and lift <u>heavy</u> things
	- Able to call for <u>help</u>
Robot costs:	New robots cost <u>a lot</u>.
	Trying to make more <u>affordable</u>.

Page 93

E

1. B   2. A   3. B   4. A

F

1. replaced   2. machine   3. workplace
4. operate   5. impressive

Practice

Page 95

C

1. A   2. A   3. B

D

1. product   2. provide   3. invented
4. computers   5. manufacture

Test

Page 96

1. C   2. A   3. D
4. B   5. B

Tesla

- (F) Found a way to send radio waves
- (D) Before him, radio waves had never been sent through the air.

Marconi

- (A) Made a radio business for ships
- (B) Was very good at science
- (C) Sent a radio message across the Atlantic

Check-up

Page 98

A

1. A   2. D

B

1. Air conditioning   2. idea   3. zippers
4. affordable   5. common   6. problems

[Unit 11]

Getting Ready

Page 100

C

3, 1, 4, 2

D

Topic:	Moldova
Introduction:	Small country in Eastern <u>Europe</u>.
	Border with <u>two</u> countries.
Weather:	Is <u>moderate</u>.
	- Warm <u>summer</u>, not hot
	- Winters not very <u>cold</u>
Farming:	Good <u>farmland</u>.
	Farmers grow fruit, which is made into <u>wine</u>.
	<u>Famous</u> for wine.
	Wine festival is in <u>October</u>.
Money:	<u>Cheap</u> to travel in.
	Not expensive to <u>buy</u> things.

Page 101

E

1. D   2. D

F

1. border   2. tropical   3. moderate
4. climate   5. traveled

Practice

Page 103

C

1. C   2. B   3. D

D

1. information   2. prevent   3. global
4. geography   5. practical

Test

Page 104

1. C   2. A   3. C   4. B
5. A   6. A, D, E

Check-up

Page 106

A

1. A

Answer Key

B

1. receivers 2. satellite 3. system
4. festival 5. Wine 6. famous

[Unit 12]

Getting Ready

Page 108

C

4, 1, 3, 2

D

Topic:	Stringed Instruments
Introduction:	Use moving strings.
	Have a <u>variety</u> of sound qualities.
	<u>Three</u> kinds.
	- <u>Arranged</u> by how they are played.
Plucked:	Plucking is <u>pulling</u> something with the fingers.
	<u>Guitars</u> are plucked.
Bowed:	Strings are moved with a <u>bow</u>.
	The bow is <u>pulled</u> across the strings.
	The violin and cello are bowed.
Struck:	Played by <u>hitting</u> the strings.
	The piano <u>possesses</u> small hammers.
	- Hit the strings to make them <u>move</u>.

Page 109

E

Plucked	Bowed	Struck
• (D) Uses fingers to move strings	• (A) Uses a special pole to move strings	• (C) Moves strings by hitting them
	• (E) Moves something across strings	• (G) Uses hammers to move strings

F

1. instrument 2. quality 3. arranged
4. possesses 5. variety

Practice

Page 111

C

1. D

2.

Sound	Scat Style	Skills
• (E) Had a cheerful style	• (A) Made up words	• (F) Sang clearly
	• (D) Used her voice as an instrument	• (I) Had excellent tone and control
• (G) Made sad songs seem happy	• (H) Tried to sound like musical instruments	

D

1. unique 2. talent 3. reputation
4. entertained 5. control

Test

Page 112

1. A 2. C 3. B 4. B
5. A 6. B, C, E

Check-up

Page 114

A

1. D

B

1. strings 2. band 3. tone
4. bow 5. hammer 6. record

[Review 2]

Reading 1

Page 115

1. B 2. D 3. D 4. B 5. C 6. B

Reading 2

Page 117

1. B 2. C 3. A 4. A 5. C 6. C

Reading 3

Page 119

1. A 2. D 3. D 4. A 5. B
6.

Causes of Diabetes
• (C) Being Overweight
• (G) Parents having diabetes

Controlling diabetes
• (A) Exercising
• (B) Eating less sugary food
• (D) Taking shots of insulin